Guide to Desktop Publishing

by
James Cavuoto
and
Stephen Beale

Graphic Arts Technical Foundation
4615 Forbes Avenue
Pittsburgh, Pennsylvania 15213-3796
Telephone: 412/621-6941
Telex: 9103509221 Fax: 412/621-3049

Paper compliments of:

Halopaque - 100 • 70-pound Vellum
100% Deinked Fiber • 15% Post Consumer

Binding compliments of
Nicholstone Companies, Inc.
Nashville, Tennessee

Product brand names are mentioned in this book as a matter of information only and does not imply endorsement by the Graphic Arts Technical Foundation.

4120924 4-92 2.5M

Contents

Foreword

For several decades, most of the changes occurring in graphic communications could be classified as being evolutionary. In the last few years, however, graphic communications has been undergoing revolutionary changes, particularly in the prepress area, where the computer is now the focal point.

Many procedures that were previously labor-intensive, such as pasteup, have been automated. The laborious task of cutting typeset galleys apart, waxing them, and carefully positioning them using a T square and triangle is no longer as common as it was just two years ago. Pasteup can now be performed electronically, using computer software called page-makeup programs.

This book, *Guide to Desktop Publishing*, gives the reader an overview of this rapidly changing area. The term "desktop publishing" encompasses a number of prepress production steps such as art and copy preparation, page makeup, and graphic arts photography. Other terms that could be used include "electronic publishing," which better describes the widespread use of computerized devices, and "desktop production," which identifies where a number of production steps are performed—the desktop of the originator of the printing job.

With conventional prepress production, each production step was performed by a different person in most cases. For example, one person might design the printed piece, another would typeset the job, a third would prepare the pasteup mechanical, and a fourth would make the line and halftone negatives for the job. With desktop publishing, fewer people are involved in the production chain. Each person now wears more than one hat, and the originator of a printing job is now responsible for more of the production operations. In some cases, one person would design the printed piece, keyboard the manuscript, paste up the job electronically, and output it directly to film.

Desktop publishing is changing so fast that we have intentionally omitted indicating the current version of the software programs mentioned in the book. Periodically, software vendors update their programs by adding or improving features. In addition, new software programs are being introduced almost daily.

Thomas M. Destree
Editor in Chief

Acknowledgments

The authors would like to thank several individuals and organizations who helped make this book possible. First and foremost, Mr. Thomas Destree, Editor in Chief at GATF, deserves recognition for his watchful editorial eye and guidance during the writing process. Several other GATF people, including Frank Benevento, Lloyd DeJidas, Dan Makuta, and Vicki Stone, were very helpful to us.

During the writing and production of the book, we made use of the following hardware products: Macintosh IIsi computer, Hewlett-Packard ScanJet IIc scanner, Microtek ScanMaker 1850s slide scanner, and a LaserMax 1000 laser printer.

The book was paginated using Aldus PageMaker version 4.2 software for the Macintosh. Final output was to film negatives produced from a high-resolution PostScript imagesetter at Color Tech Corporation in Redwood City, CA.

Introduction

When desktop publishing emerged as a new computer application in 1985, it created a revolution in the printing industry. And like most revolutionaries, the first desktop publishers confronted a bitter struggle wresting control of their own destiny from those in power.

Many graphics professionals feared that desktop publishing offered corporate and professional publishers of newsletters, books, reports, proposals, and other documents the ability to take over the means of production—page production that is. Established print shops and graphics houses resisted the advances of desktop publishing users and fought back with criticisms of the new technologies: Desktop publishing programs did not offer "true" typesetting—they lacked sophisticated typographical functions like kerning, tracking, and hyphenation. The range of available type styles was insufficient for professional users. Photographic quality was terrible.

But the quality and versatility of desktop publishing software and hardware steadily improved. One by one, the defenses thrown up by the graphics monarchy began to crumble. Programs like QuarkXPress and Aldus PageMaker added sophisticated typesetting features that rivaled the best dedicated typesetting systems. Digital font vendors such as Adobe Systems Inc. and Bitstream offered a dizzying array of typefaces and styles. And manufacturers of desktop scanners developed image scanning devices that could produce computer-generated halftone images that are virtually indistinguishable from traditional halftones.

But a funny thing happened on the way to the revolution. Rather than overthrow the printing industry, desktop publishing created a new alliance between publishing users and graphics professionals. Those businesses that adapted to the new atmosphere of computer-generated publishing found new positions of power—and profit—in the new regime.

Typesetting shops that previously railed on the inferior quality of desktop typography reoriented themselves as "desktop publishing service bureaus." Rather than perform keystroking and page formatting on their typesetting machines, service bureaus accepted diskettes containing complete desktop publishing files and produced high-resolution output on their state-of-the-art "imagesetting" machines.

Print shops that had scoffed at the quality of laser printer output actively began to recruit desktop publishing users who needed to reproduce more copies of their pages than they could do in house.

Designers and illustrators who had cringed at the artwork produced by desktop publishers now set themselves up as trainers and consultants. They offered their clients advice on how to get the most out of their graphics software programs. Or they took a design project from "rough" concept on the client's diskette to finished artwork ready for press.

Today, in spite of—or more accurately, because of—the revolution in desktop publishing, the printing and graphics industries are thriving like they never have before. Since desktop publishing makes more people publishers, more pages are produced on press. Since desktop publishing programs expose more people to concepts of typography and illustration that they never knew before, they now seek higher-quality design services. And since desktop publishing benefits printing and graphics firms as well as their clients, the industry is much more productive than it used to be.

Instead of a class struggle, the printing industry of today now enjoys peace and harmony with the growing masses of desktop publishing users.

The Purpose of This Book

We have produced this book to help the graphic arts industry stay informed on developments and products in desktop publishing. In the years ahead, we expect that both printing firms and print customers will need to become more aware of desktop publishing issues. Although we cannot cover every single product that's currently available, we intend, in the chapters that follow, to give you a broad overview of some of the key product categories that come into play.

Chapter One presents an introduction to the topic of desktop publishing. If you're new to desktop publishing, or if you need a refresher on the various elements and applications, you'll probably find this chapter useful.

In Chapter Two, we will discuss the various computer environments available for desktop publishing applications. These include the brands of personal computers as well as the graphical operating systems that run on those computers.

Chapter Three covers the first stage in the desktop publishing process: word processing. We offer descriptions of some of the key word processing products on the market, and how they interact with desktop publishing programs.

In Chapter Four, we talk about the desktop publishing programs themselves. This is the cornerstone category—these are the programs where the page layout process takes place.

Chapter Five discusses graphic illustration and drawing programs. This type of software has become very important for desktop publishing users who need to create logos, illustrations, and other types of line art for desktop publishing documents.

In Chapters Six through Eight we cover the important category of halftone imaging. We start in Chapter Six with a discussion of scanners—the digital devices that bring images into the computer. Next, in Chapter Seven, we discuss halftone image editing, where we look specifically at touching up black-and-white photographs and importing them into a publishing program. Then in Chapter Eight, we progress to color imaging, where we talk about new trends in color scanners, color separation software, calibration, and other important issues.

In Chapters Nine and Ten we complete the desktop publishing process, first with a discussion of producing output of camera-ready artwork, and then a chapter on reproducing desktop publishing documents on press.

Finally, we offer a glossary of desktop publishing terms and a listing of hardware and software manufacturers mentioned in the book.

Chapter One

Introduction to Desktop Publishing

In just a few years, desktop publishing has emerged as one of the major applications of personal computers in the world of business. Few personal computer applications have captured the imagination as has desktop publishing. Indeed, some performance claims by vendors for their desktop publishing products are based more on imagination than reality. Nevertheless, desktop publishing does give its users significant cost savings over traditional publishing. And it has permanently left its mark on the printing industry.

Using computers to prepare pages for publication is not a new phenomenon. Magazine and newspaper publishers have been using computers for editing and page layout for decades. But their computer systems cost hundreds of thousands of dollars and their customized software could cost almost as much. Until the advent of desktop publishing, the vendors of customized computer publishing systems had little incentive to produce low-cost versions of their products.

The price of a basic desktop publishing system can be as low as a few thousand dollars and can range upward to tens of thousands of dollars — an affordable range for most businesses.

What is desktop publishing? We define desktop publishing as the process of using a personal computer for most or all of the stages of publishing. The goal is to create pages that have a printed look.

The Origins of Desktop Publishing

The term "desktop publishing" was coined by Aldus Corp. president Paul Brainerd in the mid-1980s to describe an application where an inexpensive computer system, in combination with page layout software and a laser printer or imagesetter, could produce professional-looking typeset pages. For less than $10,000, a user could purchase a personal computer, laser printer, and page composition software and become a personal publishing company. Instead of pasting galleys onto a layout board, they could compose a page, complete with text and graphics, on a computer screen. Instead of sending work to a typesetting house, they could quickly and easily output it on a laser printer or imagesetter. Just as Gutenberg's invention of movable type brought books and other publications to the masses, desktop publishing made it possible for ordinary people to produce their own professional-looking documents.

Components of a Desktop Publishing System

The basic desktop system consists of a personal computer, word processing software, page layout software, and a laser printer. Software for creating or modifying illustrations and photographs, along with hardware such as a scanner that converts drawings and photographs into digitized computer files, can be part of a desktop publishing system. A mouse that

The components of a desktop publishing system: personal computer, laser printer, scanner, mouse, and software.

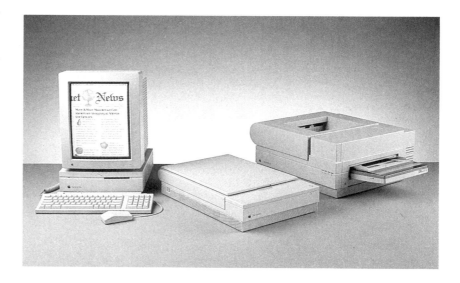

controls the cursor on the screen or a tablet for drawing and cursor control are other desirable options.

The pages produced by the laser printer can be the final "printed" product. Or a higher-resolution laser printer or "imagesetter" can produce "masters" for making plates for a printing press if hundreds or thousands of copies are needed.

Design and layout are the basic functions of page layout software. In traditional publishing, the design, layout, and pasteup are usually done by an art director, graphic designer, and their assistants.

The Traditional Publishing Process

Designing a page involves deciding how the page will look when it is printed. Professional designers use an underlying "grid" that shows where the various typographical elements — such as heads, subheads, body text, illustrations, and captions — must be placed. If the design is to be used repeatedly, the page grid is usually printed in light blue ink on stiff paper called artboards.

A layout shows how actual contents of a page will be arranged. The layout can be no more than a pencil sketch (called a "thumbnail" by professionals) or it can be a rough layout sketched directly on an artboard. If a more accurate view of the pages is required, the art director will make a comprehensive, or "comp," by pasting proofs of the text and illustrations on a board. A comp allows one to see exactly how the various elements look together and how well the text fits the pages it is to fill.

Makeup (also called pasteup) involves cutting out text and heads from proof sheets and pasting them exactly in position on boards. Line drawings can also be pasted directly on the boards as camera-ready copy. The position and size of illustrations and photographs are shown on the board, sometimes by blank spaces but more often by pasting a proof or copy of the illustration or photograph in position.

The completed boards (called mechanicals or camera-ready pages) are sent to the printer, where negatives are made with a prepress camera. The negatives of the illustrations and halftones are "stripped in" at this stage, and the combined negatives are used to make the press plates.

With desktop publishing, page design and composition are done entirely on the computer screen using page layout software. The page layout program is the heart of the desktop publishing system. With page layout software, you can specify the size and kind of type, and position it anywhere on the page. You can arrange the type in columns, or make it fit inside an arbitrary shape, say a heart. You can make changes in the text and write new text. You also can position illustrations, and alter them if needed.

The Role of PostScript

One of the key developments that made desktop publishing possible was the introduction of PostScript, a page description language from Adobe Systems. In many respects, PostScript is like other computer languages such as Basic or Pascal. But unlike other computer languages, PostScript does not run on

A PostScript program uses a series of English-like commands to describe how an image should be produced. This PostScript program generates a box.

```
%!PS-Adobe-2.0 EPSF-1.2
%%Creator: Adobe Illustrator(TM)
3.0b1r1
%%For: (Steve) (MPR)
%%Title: (ch2-7.ps)
%%CreationDate: (9/7/90) (4:49 PM)
%%DocumentProcSets:
Adobe_Illustrator_1.1 0 0
%%ColorUsage: Black&White
%%DocumentProcessColors: Black
%%BoundingBox:59 375 222 492
%%TemplateBox:288 360 288 360
%%TileBox:0 0 552 730
%%DocumentPreview: None
%%EndComments
%%EndProlog
%%BeginSetup
%%EndSetup
u
0.5 g
0 G
0 i 0 J 0 j 1 w 4 M []0 d
%%Note:
220 377 m
220 490 L
61 490 L
61 377 L
220 377 L
b
140.5 433.5 m
B
U
%%Trailer
```

your computer. Rather, it runs on an output device such as a laser printer or imagesetter.

It is not necessary to understand how PostScript works in order to use its power and flexibility. You need only use your publishing software the way you normally do to access the full range of PostScript functions. Nonetheless, it is worthwhile to have a limited understanding of how the page description language works.

The most important thing to understand about PostScript is that it is a programming language with all the power and flexibility of languages that run on computers. Unlike general-purpose computer languages, PostScript has one main function: to produce images in the form of dots on an output device. It uses English-like commands that can create almost any kind of graphic image or text a user might desire.

Because it is a programming language, a user can theoretically write a PostScript program to produce pages. If we had wanted, we could have written this entire book as a PostScript program. However, this is not very practical; writing PostScript programs requires considerable training and skill. However, most desktop publishing and graphics programs have the ability to generate PostScript files. Sometimes this is handled by the program itself. In other cases, it is handled by the general system software.

When you print a file on a PostScript laser printer or imagesetter, your software generates a PostScript program and sends it to the output device. There, a controller or raster image processor (RIP) converts the commands in the PostScript program into instructions that guide the printer as it produces the page. If you were to print the output to a disk file, you would be able to open it with a word processor and see the PostScript commands used to produce the page.

PostScript is particularly worthwhile for desktop and professional publishing users. There are many reasons for this, including font quality, typeface variety, picture quality, device independence, and support for publishing software.

Desktop Publishing Applications

What can you do with desktop publishing? Perhaps the best way to acquaint you with the performance capabilities of a desktop publishing system is to describe some typical business and office applications.

Illustrated Reports

One common application of desktop publishing in the office is the production of lengthy reports that include many tables, graphs, and other illustrations. Usually these reports are updates of one that was produced previously. Since the introduction of personal computers, updating and writing such reports can be done quickly and efficiently using word processing, spreadsheet, and database software.

However, when the text and tables and illustrations are sent to the printer, the office staff can be subjected to weeks of agony as they try to catch all the errors introduced by the typesetter and the page-makeup operators. Inevitably, despite their efforts, the printed report will probably contain errors in the final stages, such as transposed columns in tables, mislabeled maps, and graphs without legends.

With desktop publishing, when the time comes to produce the report, the primary text proofing and data checking are done by the staff at the word processing stage. Graphs are prepared directly from the database using the graph-making software, so the data should be correct. A scanner is used to digitize photographs and illustrations. The material text and illustrations are imported into the page layout program and formatted into pages.

Proofs produced by the laser printer enable the staff to scrutinize and correct each page until it has no errors. The fast turnaround at this stage is a major benefit of using desktop publishing.

Product Literature

Another application is keeping product literature up to date. Spec sheets, for example, change frequently for some product lines. With traditional publishing methods, the production of spec sheets is both expensive and time-consuming. With desktop publishing, one operator can keep the spec sheets for several product lines up to date. Revisions that take weeks in traditional publishing can be made in less than a day. The laser-printed pages can be sent to the printer as "camera-ready" copy, or they can serve as masters for making photocopies if the spec sheets are needed immediately.

Newsletters

An early use of desktop publishing was for the production of newsletters, particularly staff newsletters. With traditional publishing methods, it usually takes five to seven days to get the newsletter typeset and printed after all the text has been received. With desktop publishing, the production process is accelerated and can be completed in one day.

Stories for the newsletter can be written by various company employees using a standard word processing program. The newsletter editor can collect all of the stories and items on his or her computer's hard disk. After all of the stories for the issue are on hand, the text is imported by the page-makeup program into templates for each page of the newsletter. The text flows into the appropriate areas.

The laser-printed page proofs can be circulated to upper management for approval. If changes or corrections are needed, they can be made quickly and new proofs printed out. When final approval is obtained, the formatted pages can be copied onto a floppy disk and sent to the printer for typesetting. The pages created by the typesetting equipment are identical to those created on the laser printer, but higher in resolution.

Catalogs

Catalogs are another type of publication that are well-suited for production using desktop publishing. The traditional method of individually pasting illustrations and type in position to prepare camera-ready pages is extremely tedious. Even minor changes can be very expensive. With a page layout program, the catalog pages, including text and illustrations, can be composed and manipulated on the computer screen. Page proofs produced by the laser printer are much less expensive than traditional page proofs. Changes do not require cut and paste, but just altering digitized text and images on the screen. Production cost savings are high, and turnaround time is much faster. If the format of the catalog remains unchanged, desktop publishing can be used to create revisions and updates in a matter of days instead of weeks.

Cost of Desktop Publishing

Desktop publishing systems are more expensive than the basic office personal computer systems that are used for word processing, spreadsheets, and databases. A desktop publishing computer should have more memory and faster operating speed than the average office computer, which means a higher cost computer. A large display screen is desirable, and that adds to the cost. A laser printer is essential and probably will cost more than the computer. Then there is the additional cost of the page layout software, graphics, draw, paint, and image processing software, and perhaps a scanner for digitizing photographs and illustrations.

In addition, there is the cost of training personnel to use the new hardware and software, and perhaps a continuing outlay for a full-time employee to operate the desktop publishing system.

But when the capital and operating costs of a desktop publishing system are compared to the cost of producing the same items using traditional publishing methods, the return on investment for the desktop publishing system can be astounding, particularly for printed products that are frequently revised.

Benefits of Desktop Publishing

Although the potential cost savings play an important part in the decision to use desktop publishing, these savings are not always the major benefits that are experienced after the system is in operation.

For some desktop publishing users, control over the typesetting and page-makeup operations is the most important benefit. This is particularly true for publishers of technical and financial documents that typically have to be altered just before going to press.

Desktop publishing can reduce the time it takes to correct the type of errors that are introduced by the traditional typesetting and page-makeup process. These errors include spelling mistakes, omission of words or entire lines, poor word spacing, and undesirable hyphenation. These potential errors make it necessary to proofread the typeset text each time corrections are made. Of course, careful proofreading and copyediting are still required in desktop publishing, but the proofreading is done on screen or with laser-printed proofs. Corrections can be proofread immediately instead of having to wait for new proofs to arrive from the printing plant.

With desktop publishing, text and numbers can be checked and double-checked at the word processing stage until most of the errors have been corrected. This corrected copy is then transferred directly into the page layout. Because the number of typos and other errors are likely to be few, proofing laser-printed pages is quick. Also changes to copy at the layout stage do not usually create problems. A new page proof takes only a few minutes.

Being able to see instantly on screen what the printed page

will look like gives the desktop publishing user the opportunity to make improvements or to change the design without incurring typesetting and page pasteup costs. Page proofs from a laser printer usually give a very close approximation of what the typeset version will look like, and in many instances the laser printed pages can themselves serve as the "camera-ready" copy for the printer.

With no intermediaries between the approved version and the copy photographed by the printer's camera, the chances for the introduction of typos, transpositions, and other production errors are reduced to almost nil. This control over the production process can by itself justify the installation of the desktop system.

Fast turnaround time is regarded as the primary benefit of desktop publishing, particularly by sales and promotion managers who usually have very short lead times for producing printed material. Using traditional publishing methods, fast turnaround always translates into overtime and high costs, sometimes six to eight times higher than normal cost.

With desktop publishing, fast turnaround is possible at a reasonable cost, or in some instances at no increase at all in the cost because desktop publishing does not require the coordinated efforts of a series of specialized workers such as typesetters, page layout and pasteup artists, and the page-makeup specialists at the printing plant. All the changes can be done by the operator of the desktop publishing equipment.

Another benefit of desktop publishing is the saving of personal time, particularly for the managers who are responsible for the contents and production of the printed material. The round-robin sequences of traditional publishing are time-consuming and inefficient. Desktop publishing has freed its users from the drudgery of repeated proofreading required in traditional publishing—mainly to catch typos and errors introduced by the production process.

Finally, the cost saving can also be significant, particularly the saving in typesetting costs. Desktop publishing opened the way to typesetting complete pages instead of just text. A page composed on a desktop publishing system should have to be output only once on typesetting paper after it is approved. All the corrections can be made before the page is sent to the typesetter. There are additional savings in the cost of page layout and the final composing of the page with text and illustrations.

Pitfalls of Desktop Publishing

Enthusiasm for desktop publishing is contagious, and proselytizers gloss over the shortcomings and limitations. Almost anyone who can operate a personal computer can learn to use a desktop publishing system. But desktop publishing requires more than just the skill to operate a computer — it requires verbal and artistic skills to produce readable and visually pleasing printed pages. A major pitfall of desktop publishing is that it can give the user the false assurance that the hardware and software are adequate substitutes for skill and talent. Some horrible examples of printing have been produced by desktop publishers who seem to be blind to visual aesthetics. Every company that introduces desktop publishing into its operations should establish graphic guidelines and standards for all printed material. Otherwise, the desktop publishing system could lead to the creation of a typographical tower of Babel.

Any company or office that is setting up a desktop publishing system also must take into account the personnel that will be required to operate the system. Often, that will mean having to hire one or more persons with some knowledge and skill in print production. Failure to staff a desktop operation properly will result in poor quality output, higher operating costs, and perhaps even lead to the abandonment of the investment because of the inadequate results.

In choosing hardware and software, the primary pitfall to avoid is incompatibility. Some pieces of equipment will not function together, and there are application programs that will not work well together on a computer. So the key question when selecting hardware and software is: Will it work smoothly with all of the other components of my system?

In the next chapter, we'll start the process of assembling a desktop publishing system by looking at the various computer environments that support desktop publishing.

Chapter Two

Computer Environments

For most users, the process of creating pages begins with a computer system equipped with publishing, graphics, and word processing software. These systems, known as "front ends," are usually Macintosh or IBM-compatible microcomputers. In this chapter, we will explore the front-end environments most often used in desktop publishing applications. We'll begin by covering the two principal hardware platforms, Apple's Macintosh and the IBM compatibles. In our discussion of IBM compatibles, we'll look at graphical operating environments like Microsoft Windows and GEM that offer many of the user-friendly advantages of the Apple machine. The chapter concludes with a discussion of software packages frequently used to produce pages, including graphics and desktop publishing programs.

Hardware Platforms

The choice of a hardware platform is important, because it dictates the range of software from which you will be able to select. Most businesses are well stocked with IBM-compatible machines, so they will naturally lean toward that standard. But others may want to consider the Macintosh for its easy learning curve and graphical capabilities. Then again, you can stick with the IBM clones and purchase a graphical operating environment like Microsoft Windows that provides many Macintosh-like capabilities, or wait for the new OS/2 or Unix standards to emerge in the next few years with their particular advantages.

A little history is in order. The IBM PC standard was born in 1981 when IBM released its first Personal Computer, which ran under an operating system called DOS (for disk operating system), developed by Microsoft Corp. DOS, like any other operating system, is a set of programs that handle the basic housekeeping chores required to run a computer system. In

Most DOS programs use a character-based interface. The screen is a grid of 80 columns and 25 lines in which each intersecting point can contain a single character.

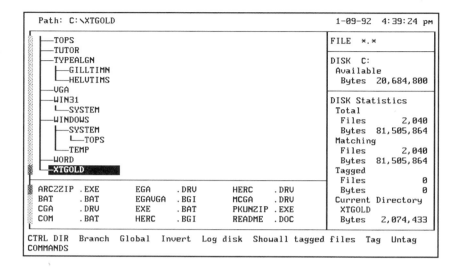

addition to providing commands for copying, deleting, and organizing computer files, it serves as an intermediary between the computer hardware and applications software (including word-processing packages). Programs must be written specifically to work with a particular operating system, though they can be adapted to work with other systems as well.

DOS received some of its inspiration from an early operating system known as CP/M, which was developed by a company called Digital Research. CP/M was the first microcomputer operating system that was not proprietary to a particular manufacturer's system. Instead, manufacturers could license the operating system for their machines, and many did so. The popularity of CP/M machines created an attractive user base for software developers, causing a proliferation of business-oriented CP/M programs. These included early versions of software packages that remain popular to this day, including WordStar and dBase.

IBM's PC and its DOS operating system improved on CP/M in many ways, providing a platform for the development of more powerful software packages. By 1984, CP/M computers were well on their way to oblivion, and DOS was the reigning computer standard. Many companies established thriving businesses selling computers known as IBM "compatibles" or "clones," which also operated under DOS and could run the same software packages as the PC. DOS became so entrenched that nearly all software packages developed for microcomputers were compatible with it.

As popular as it was (and still is), DOS had many limitations.

It is essentially a command-driven system. To use its features, you must memorize a set of commands for copying and deleting files, setting up your hard disk, or performing other system chores. Programs are generally run by typing in their name. This approach makes the system more difficult to learn and use than other interfaces we'll discuss later.

Graphical User Interfaces

Most DOS programs also use what might be called a "text-based" interface. The basic screen is a matrix of 80 columns and 25 lines in which each intersecting point can contain a single character. Users interact with the programs through the keyboard by typing in commands or making selections from a menu of options. For certain types of commands, they may have to hit function keys or hold down the Control or Alt keys in conjunction with another character. Many of these programs provide a

A mouse is a small hand-held device connected by cable to the computer. Moving the mouse on the desktop causes corresponding movement of the cursor on the computer screen.

great deal of power, but again, this text-based orientation often makes them difficult to learn and use.

When Apple released its ill-fated Lisa computer in 1982, it introduced a new kind of operating system that used what's

A bit-mapped display is composed of tiny dots that can be turned on or off individually, allowing the computer to show graphic images in addition to text.

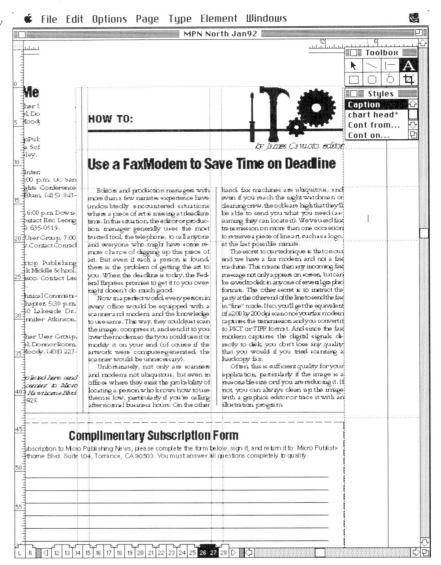

known as a "graphical interface." This approach, actually pioneered by Xerox Corp. at its Palo Alto Research Center, allows development of software that is generally easier to learn and use than packages developed for text-based interfaces.

Two essential elements in this kind of interface are a "mouse" and a "bit-mapped display." A mouse is a small hand-held device connected by cable to the computer. Moving the mouse around the desktop causes corresponding movement of the cursor on the computer screen. Files can be moved, programs run, and commands executed merely by moving the mouse to the appropriate location and hitting a button (an action known in mouse parlance as "clicking"). A bit-mapped display, unlike a text-based display, is composed of tiny dots that can be turned on or off individually, allowing the computer to show graphic images in addition to text. The typical Macintosh display has a screen resolution of about 72 dots per inch (dpi). This is no match for the 300-dpi resolution of most laser printers, but it is sufficient for displaying many kinds of images.

Graphical interfaces are easy to use because they allow an intuitive "point and click" approach to software operation. Files and software functions are displayed as small graphical icons, such as a book to represent a text file, or a magnifying glass for a software function that allows you to zoom in on a portion of the screen. Instead of typing commands, you can point the cursor at an icon or menu selection and click. Graphical interfaces are also characterized by their use of "windows," frames on the computer screen in which different files can be displayed.

Apple's Lisa was slow and expensive, and it suffered an early demise. But Apple used the same graphical interface approach in its highly successful Macintosh computer, released in 1984. The early Macs had insufficient memory and disk storage for serious business applications, so software developers were slow to introduce programs for the machine. But its graphical orientation and ease of use made it popular among artists and college students, and it gradually caught on in the business world as well. Apple steadily enhanced the machine, adding memory, disk storage, and other features while promoting its merits among software publishers.

Desktop Publishing on the Macintosh

As we saw above, the Macintosh's graphical user interface was an important innovation. But the Macintosh was also the first operating environment to support PostScript. Apple's LaserWriter printer, introduced in 1985, was one of the first PostScript printers available. The combination of PostScript and the computer's built-in graphics capabilities made the Macintosh a natural choice for publishing applications, and it remains popular among desktop publishing and computer graphics users.

Any model of the Macintosh can produce output on a PostScript printer or imagesetter as long as the printer is equipped with an AppleTalk port. This connector is both physically and electronically distinct from the serial or parallel interface ports used by

Apple's Macintosh, introduced in 1984, has grown into a family of computers that are popular among desktop publishing users.

other types of computer printers. The AppleTalk connection allows the Macintosh to communicate with PostScript printers at a rate of 230,000 bits per second—more than 20 times faster than the serial communication used by other computers. It also allows the output device to operate on the AppleTalk network, so that many users can share the printer. To connect a PostScript printer to the AppleTalk network, you must purchase an AppleTalk connector kit for the printer and for each Macintosh you would like to use on the network.

Apple Macintosh users enjoy a special advantage with respect to PostScript: nearly every software application that runs on the Macintosh computer can produce PostScript output. The reason for this is that Apple engineers built PostScript support into its standard printer "driver," a term that refers to the software that manages printing operations. Any application that fully conforms to the Macintosh operating system automatically supports PostScript. There is no need for the software developer to write a special PostScript driver.

The standard Macintosh driver supports several key areas of PostScript output, including:

- Fonts

- Object graphics

- Bit-mapped graphics

- Network performance

Fonts

The Macintosh supports an unlimited number of fonts and a nearly infinite selection of point sizes for each font. Once you have installed a font in the system file of your Macintosh, all of your applications will have access to it. In most applications, you select your choice of fonts, type style, and point size from menu options labeled Font, Format, or Style.

Object Graphics

Computer systems generally support two types of graphic images: object graphics and bit-mapped graphics. Object graphics are elements such as circles, lines, rectangles, and shading patterns produced by drawing programs such as MacDraw or SuperPaint, which are discussed in greater detail later in this chapter. When sent to the printer, each graphic element is converted from its internal Macintosh representation into the appropriate PostScript language command. This ensures that object graphics will be imaged at the maximum resolution of the PostScript printer or imagesetter. Thus, circles or rectangles that appear jagged on the Macintosh display will appear smooth on output.

Object graphics can also be enlarged or reduced without loss of quality. For example, if you import a drawing produced in MacDraw into PageMaker and then enlarge it by a factor of two, the image will not lose any quality when sent to your PostScript printer.

Bit-Mapped Graphics

Bit-mapped graphics are the paint-type images created with such programs as MacPaint or FullPaint, or captured by means of a scanner. These images are sent on a dot-for-dot basis from the Macintosh to your PostScript printer. As a result, they will not appear any better in printed form than they did on screen. Also, if you enlarge a bit-mapped image at output time, the effective resolution of the printed image will be diminished. These types of images are discussed in greater detail later in this chapter.

Network Performance

The print manager software built into the Macintosh system not only handles the font and graphic conversions discussed above, but it also manages the details of getting pages from the Macintosh to the PostScript output device. In a network environment, with many users seeking access to the printer at the same time, this is not a straightforward task. Each time a Macintosh user tries to print, the computer transmits a message over the AppleTalk network to see if the chosen output device is available. If so, it sends the PostScript commands that represent each page of output over the AppleTalk network to the printer. If the printer is not available or is in use by another network user, the Macintosh sends an appropriate message to the user.

If a print spooling program like Apple's PrintMonitor is installed, you needn't wait for the computer to send all of the PostScript commands to the printer. You also needn't worry about someone else using the printer at the same time. Instead of sending output directly to the printer, the Macintosh will send it to a disk file. This disk file will be printed when the output device becomes available; the computer can still be used while printing takes place.

PostScript Printing Options

PostScript printers offer several unique options for Macintosh users. At print time, you can elect to enlarge or reduce your printed pages by a specified percentage. PostScript handles all the details of producing text and graphic images in the proper sizes without compromising image quality. You can also choose to invert your output so that a mirror image is produced. This is useful for certain photographic options in lithography. Similarly, you may choose to produce a photographic negative of your pages, so that black becomes white and vice versa. Again, this is useful for producing images directly on film, a process that can save you the cost of camera work during offset reproduction.

Applications that Support PostScript Directly

The capabilities described above are available to any Macintosh user with the standard built-in printer driver. As powerful as this driver is, it does not tap the full potential of the PostScript language. For this reason, a growing number of Macintosh applications support PostScript directly and offer graphic effects beyond the capabilities of Apple's print driver. These effects are still available only if you have a PostScript output device. They include text rotation, gray-scale imaging, color imaging, and fill and fountain effects.

Desktop Publishing with an IBM-Compatible

The IBM PC and compatible computers represent the most popular computer environment available today. Unlike the Macintosh, where a single company—Apple Computer—is responsible for manufacturing the computer and developing the system software, the IBM environment is a free-for-all where no single company has absolute control. IBM, which developed the original IBM Personal Computer, no longer manufactures that particular computer. However, many other companies make computers compatible with the PC and its successors, the XT and AT. IBM offers a line of microcomputers known collectively as the Personal System/2, which are in many ways incompatible with the older machines.

The most influential company in terms of IBM-compatible software is Microsoft, which developed the DOS operating system and is also a major developer of applications software. Still, the IBM-compatible environment lacks the kind of conformity made possible in the Macintosh environment where a single company has control. This situation, as we shall see, has benefits and drawbacks.

IBM-compatible computers connect with output devices through one of four interface ports: serial, parallel, AppleTalk, or the optional Ethernet interface. AppleTalk or Ethernet connections are used when the computer is part of a local-area network; they represent the fastest form of communication, but are also the most expensive because you must install a network interface card in the computer. The serial or parallel interfaces

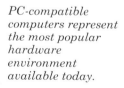

PC-compatible computers represent the most popular hardware environment available today.

are used when a single computer is connected to the printer. However, serial connections tend to be very slow.

To take full advantage of the graphics capabilities in PostScript, an IBM-compatible computer must have a bit-mapped display. In a bit-mapped display system, the software controls each dot on the screen individually, allowing the computer to show graphic images in addition to text. The Macintosh includes a built-in bit-mapped display with 72 dpi. The standard DOS display, on the other hand, is limited to showing characters in an 80-column by 25-line grid. But through a standard graphics display adapter, such as Hercules, CGA, EGA, or VGA, you can add bit-mapped display capabilities to an IBM-compatible computer. Almost all monochrome monitors sold with IBM compatibles include a Hercules-compatible adapter. Most color monitors are sold with a VGA adapter.

One problem with IBM-compatible computers is that many people find the DOS operating system difficult to use. To master DOS, you need to learn a series of commands that are entered from the keyboard. For this reason, some software developers have designed graphical user interfaces (GUIs) that provide PC users with environments offering many of the advantages of the Macintosh. Like the Macintosh with its standard printer driver, the DOS-based GUIs provide built-in drivers that support PostScript output. Software written to run under these interfaces can provide the same kind of access to PostScript's powerful graphics features found in the Macintosh. The difference is that much of the work of implementing this PostScript support is left to the individual software developer rather than being handled system-wide.

The most widely used GUI is Microsoft Windows. Others include GEM, from Digital Research, and the OS/2 Presentation Manager, also from Microsoft. In general, these environments work only with software packages that have been written specifically for them. For example, you cannot run the Windows version of Ventura Publisher under the GEM interface.

In addition to these standard operating environments, many developers offer stand-alone applications that can produce PostScript output. Some of these applications run under their own graphical environments, while others, primarily word processing programs, run under the DOS character-based interface.

Microsoft Windows

Microsoft Windows is the most popular graphical operating environment for DOS computers. The early versions of the system suffered from slow performance and memory management problems, but these have been addressed with later versions of the environment beginning with Windows version 3, which was introduced in 1990. Many developers of desktop publishing and graphics programs for the Macintosh offer versions of their packages for Windows.

Microsoft Windows includes a driver for PostScript output. As a result, nearly any program that works with Windows can produce output on a PostScript output device. Windows also offers functions that allow the user to install screen and printer fonts. Printer fonts are automatically loaded when the user installs the output device. As with the Macintosh, users can install an unlimited number of fonts and point sizes. Again, this is handled through the Windows Control Panel. Once the font is installed, it is available to all Windows applications. However, you can also install fonts that are application-specific and work only with a particular program, such as the Corel Draw illustration package.

Like the Macintosh, Windows supports a wide range of capabilities in graphics and desktop publishing applications, including object-oriented and bit-mapped images. However, the operating system places more responsibility on individual

Microsoft Windows is the most popular graphical operating environment for DOS computers.

applications to perform many software operations that are handled system-wide on the Macintosh.

This reliance on individual applications also carries over to network software. On installation, Windows can automatically detect the presence of a local-area network. However, it does not offer built-in functions for handling user conflicts and other networking issues that are handled by the Macintosh system software. Instead, these tasks are performed by the specific network operating system installed alongside Windows.

GEM

The GEM environment, from Digital Research Inc., is one of the oldest graphical environments for IBM-compatible computers. One of the most popular programs that runs under GEM is the DOS edition of Ventura Publisher (which is also available in Windows and Macintosh versions). The advantage of GEM is that users of less powerful machines such as the IBM XT and compatibles can use a graphical environment without a severe performance penalty. Besides Ventura Publisher, other popular programs that run under GEM include Finesse, a low-cost publishing program from Logitech, and Per:Form, a forms design program from Delrina Technology.

Like Windows, GEM includes a PostScript printer driver that is available to any application that runs under the environment. However, some GEM programs, such as Ventura Publisher, incorporate their own PostScript drivers that enhance output quality and performance.

The DOS version of Ventura Publisher runs under the GEM graphical environment from Digital Research.

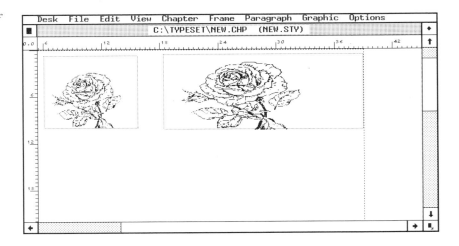

OS/2 Presentation Manager

OS/2 is the next-generation operating system announced by IBM in 1988 and manufactured by Microsoft. The Presentation Manager is a version of OS/2 that incorporates a GUI very similar to that in Microsoft Windows. OS/2 requires more memory than Windows, but it has many new capabilities of interest to desktop publishing and graphics users. Among these are the ability to run several applications simultaneously, and to have those applications share information among themselves while they are running.

Stand-Alone Applications

Aside from the three graphical operating environments we discussed above, many stand-alone applications for the IBM PC and compatibles can be used to produce desktop-published pages. Most word processing programs that run under a character-based interface on DOS offer PostScript output as an option. The problem with many of these programs is that you don't get a good idea of how your pages will look until they are printed. In many cases, files created by a word processing program will be imported into page layouts created with a desktop publishing package that runs under GEM or Windows. In addition to character-based programs, some PostScript-compatible software packages run under their own proprietary graphical environments.

Unix Workstation Environments

Most of this book focuses on electronic publishing with Macintosh and IBM-compatible computers. But many Unix-based workstations also run desktop publishing software. Unix was originally developed as a science-oriented operating system for university and engineering environments, but it is steadily building up a core of mainstream business applications.

Manufacturers of Unix-based workstations include Sun Microsystems, Hewlett-Packard, and NeXT Computers. The two most popular Unix-based publishing packages are Interleaf Publisher and FrameMaker. These are high-performance programs oriented toward high-volume publishers of books, technical manuals, and proposals.

Application Software

So far, we have focused our discussion on computer hardware and system software. But it is the application software—word processing, graphics, desktop publishing, and so on—that makes a computer system truly useful. Almost any kind of program, including spreadsheets, databases, and statistical analysis software, can play a part in the desktop publishing process. But certain categories of software play an especially important role in producing pages. The three most important categories are bit-mapped graphics software, object-oriented graphics software, and desktop publishing software.

Bit-Mapped Graphics

As mentioned above, graphic images produced on a computer system fall into two general categories: bit-mapped and object-oriented. Bit-mapped images, simply defined, are images pro-

Paint programs, such as SuperPaint, produce images in the form of dots.

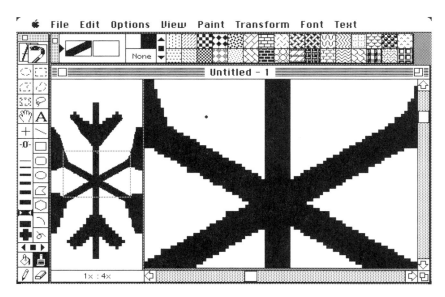

duced as a pattern of dots. They are sometimes described as "pixel-oriented," "raster," or "paint" images. Images displayed on a computer screen are bit-mapped. The Macintosh display, for example, shows images at a resolution of 72 dpi. Laser printers and imagesetters also produce bit-mapped images, laser printers at 300 dpi and imagesetters at resolutions of up to 3000 dpi or more. At that resolution it is impossible to see the individual dots, but the images are bit-mapped all the same.

Bit-mapped graphics programs come in many varieties.

Simple paint programs allow you to create pictures, or retouch scanned images in black and white or a limited number of colors. They typically include a paintbrush, eraser, paint bucket, and a selection of different patterns, colors, and line widths. Most include a zoom-in mode that allows you to edit individual pixels. They are generally easy to use, but they are also limited in the kinds of images they can produce. One limitation is resolution. Some can produce images with up to 300 dpi, but others are limited to 72 dpi.

Image-editing programs are designed to work with black-and-white photographs and other images with multiple shades of gray. At first glance, they seem much like paint packages, with many of the same tools and other similar features. However, they also include features that allow you to manipulate the gray value of each pixel in an image. Some can produce photographic effects previously achieved only in a darkroom.

Illustration programs use object-oriented graphics tools to produce artwork that can be printed at high resolutions.

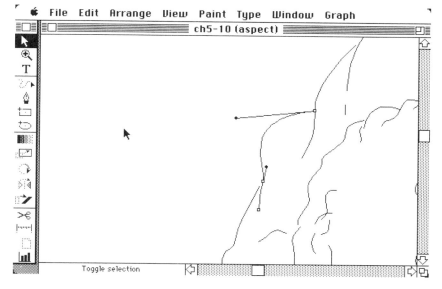

We will describe these packages more extensively in Chapter Seven.

Color image-editing programs take image editing a step further and allow you to work with color photographs and other images in which the intensity of individual colors can vary. They tend to be quite sophisticated and can be used to produce visual effects that once were possible only on expensive color workstations. These programs will be discussed more extensively in Chapter Eight.

Illustration Programs

The second kind of image is known as a "draw" or "object-oriented" graphic, and it is generally created by a category of software known as draw or illustration programs. True to their name, object-oriented graphics programs treat images as collections of discrete objects. The basic units of these objects are lines and curves. Once lines and curves are used to create an object, the object can be combined and arranged with other objects to create complex illustrations. You can also fill objects with specified colors or shades of gray.

Objects in a paint program are rendered as a pattern of bits, but objects in a draw program are described mathematically. To produce a circle, for example, a draw program uses a mathematical expression that translates into a circle on the screen, and later on the page. Because the image is not locked into a particular bit pattern, it can be printed at the full resolution of

Desktop publishing programs combine text and images created with other software packages.

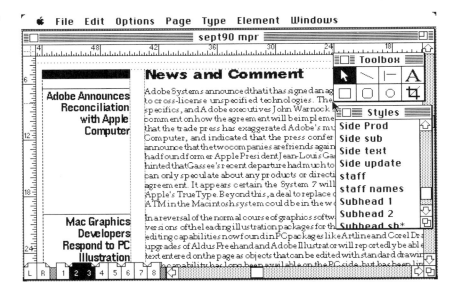

the output device, whether a 300-dpi laser printer or 2540-dpi imagesetter. We mentioned earlier that monitors and output devices produce images as patterns of bits. This is still true of object-oriented images. The difference is that the software internally recognizes the objects as mathematical expressions. It is only when the image is displayed or printed that it is converted to the bit-mapped format.

Draw programs allow artists to create complex illustrations with great precision. Because the software recognizes lines and curves as distinct objects, they can be stretched, moved, rotated, or manipulated in other ways. Small objects can be grouped into larger objects, which can also be manipulated.

Most programs in this category use what are known as Bezier curves. Such curves can be moved, resized, and reshaped by means of small handles that appear on or near the curve. These handles are known as control points. Bezier curves permit a great deal of flexibility and control over the slope and length of curves, but using them effectively to create objects takes practice. Most illustration programs have a freehand feature that allows you to draw a curve, then inserts endpoints and anchor points that can be further manipulated. We will cover illustration programs in more detail in Chapter Five.

Desktop Publishing Packages

For most users, desktop publishing packages are the principal means of producing publications. These programs, also known as page layout or page composition packages, allow users to create a wide range of publications using desktop computers. Typically, the user is shown an on-screen representation of a page layout on which text and graphics can be positioned. Most desktop publishing programs have limited tools for creating text and graphics. Instead, they are designed to incorporate text and graphics created with other programs. For example, a user might use a word processing package like Microsoft Word to write articles, a paint program like SuperPaint to create bit-mapped images, and an illustration program like Aldus Freehand to produce object-oriented images. These elements are then imported into the desktop publishing program and positioned on the page.

Desktop publishing programs vary widely in their functions and capabilities. Low-end packages are suited mostly for producing flyers and other simple one-page documents. More complex publishing packages include sophisticated features like style sheets, indexing, and typographic functions that offer precise control over character spacing. Some word processing packages have page layout and graphics import features that approach the functionality of desktop publishing software. At the same time, many desktop publishing programs are adding features like spell checking and find-and-replace that were once the province of word processing packages.

Almost all desktop publishing packages are capable of producing PostScript output. In fact, you can write an article or create a graphic image in a program that does not support

PostScript, then import it into a publishing package for output on a PostScript laser printer or imagesetter. Some of these programs use the standard PostScript driver provided with the operating environment. Others include their own PostScript drivers that add capabilities not found in the standard driver.

Chapter Three

Word Processing

Word processing is one of the most popular microcomputer applications, accounting for a large percentage of all software packages purchased each year. These programs, which simplify the process of creating written documents, have revolutionized the office environment, reducing even the fanciest electronic typewriters to museum pieces in just a few years.

Word processing packages are significant to desktop publishing because they are the primary means of entering text into page-makeup programs. After text has been entered using word processing software, it can be formatted and assembled with a page-makeup program. It is important to select a word processing program that is fully supported by the page-makeup software that will be used. However, nearly any page-makeup program can import text-only files from almost all word processing programs.

Word processing packages vary tremendously in price, features, and performance. Some are relatively simple and inexpensive, aiming themselves at users who want to produce memos, letters, and reports without investing a lot of learning time. Others are sophisticated tools for producing books and technical reports with footnotes, tables, indices, and tables of contents. Some use the traditional PC-type display, requiring that the user employ function keys or control-key combinations to invoke the program's features. Others, especially the packages that run on Apple's Macintosh, use a graphical interface that makes the program easy to use and more capable of displaying a realistic representation of how pages will be printed.

The word processing market is fiercely competitive. One vendor will release a package that includes new features, only to find them imitated in new versions of competitors' software. Many of the leading programs on the market, such as MacWrite,

A graphical user interface, such as Microsoft Windows, lets you see a realistic representation of how a document will appear in printed form.

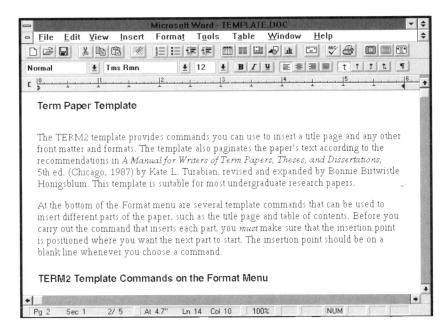

Microsoft Word, and WordPerfect, have been around for years, but regular upgrades and revisions have made them far more capable than their original releases. The ultimate winner of these "feature wars," of course, is the user.

The latest round of features to appear in word processing packages is largely the result of the growing popularity of laser printers. Back when the choice of output devices was between letter-quality daisywheel printers and correspondence-quality dot-matrix printers, word processing users did not have to worry about things like fonts and graphics. Now that laser printers are the norm in many offices, word processing packages have added many of the capabilities found in desktop publishing programs, including the ability to select fonts and incorporate graphic images. This, in turn, has reinforced the importance of the WYSIWYG (what you see is what you get) display. No longer is it sufficient for a word processor to show you a rough approximation of which characters will go on which lines. Instead, many packages now let you see a realistic representation of how a document will appear in printed form, including images and multiple-column layouts.

Just having a lot of features, however, does not necessarily guarantee a successful word processing product. The best packages are able to integrate their myriad features in a way that simplifies the learning process and maximizes productivity. This is the sort of intangible aspect of using software that

*Some word
processing
programs, such as
Microsoft Word for
DOS, use pull-down
menus.*

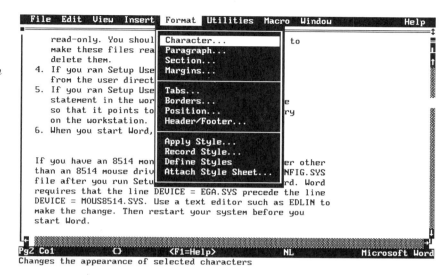

cannot be determined from merely reading a list of technical specifications, but which must be evaluated from hands-on use of the product.

In this chapter, we will profile leading word processing programs that are often used in conjunction with page-makeup software. But first, let's explore the various characteristics that distinguish one word processing program from another.

Software Features

In terms of software features, word processing packages tend to fall into one of two categories. "Managerial" or "executive" word processors are relatively inexpensive packages that emphasize ease of use and learning, but sacrifice some of the sophisticated features, like indexing and cross-references, found in more expensive programs. These include Professional Write in the DOS environment and MacWrite and WriteNow on the Macintosh. "Professional-level" word processors offer a wide range of document production features, but are costlier and more difficult to learn than the managerial packages. They include Microsoft Word and WordPerfect, which are available for both Macintosh and DOS computers.

Beyond this key distinction, features found in word processing packages fall into several basic categories. Editing features such as cut-and-paste and block deletion are found in just about every program. All packages also offer formatting features that allow you to define margins, indents, tabs, page breaks and other settings. Some offer powerful formatting tools known as style sheets that can dramatically improve productivity. Document management features include indexing, footnotes, cross-references, table-of-contents generation, and redlining. Most packages offer indexing functions, but other features like redlining and cross-references are found largely in the professional-level programs. Writing aids such as spell-checking and an on-line thesaurus are relatively common. All packages provide output features like printing and mail-merge, but some are better than others in their support for a wide range of output devices. Finally, some packages offer "extras" like mathematical calculations and sorting.

It should be repeated that features alone do not distinguish a superior word processor from an inferior one. Also important is the way a particular package interacts with the user. While Macintosh applications use the same general graphical interface, DOS programs differ in how they provide access to their features. Some, like Microsoft Word, use menu-like structure where you hit a key that provides access to a list of functions. Others, like WordPerfect, rely on function keys to invoke commands. Still others, such as WordStar, use control-key combinations. One recent phenomenon is the emergence of word processing packages that run under Windows. These programs, which include Microsoft Word for Windows, WordStar for Windows, and Ami Professional, offer many of the same advantages found in the Macintosh packages.

The particular approach used by a package has much to do with how easy it will be to learn or use. WordStar, for example, uses different control-key combinations to delete a character, word, line, or block of text. To delete a character, you type "G" while holding the control key; to delete a word, you type Control-T. These key combinations may be hard to remember, but once you have them memorized you can edit a document very quickly. Other programs require that you highlight a section of text, then hit a delete key. This is intuitive and easy to learn, but WordStar users may find it clumsy compared with their program's method.

Editing Features

Editing functions represent the core of the typical word processing package. These are the features that allow you to add and delete characters, words, lines, and blocks from your document. They also include search-and-replace and cut-and-paste functions.

Cut-and-paste functions allow you to select a block of text

and move it or copy it to a new location. The user generally highlights a section, then issues a command to copy or move the text to a new location. Because the Macintosh uses a standard cut-and-paste method across all applications, you can usually cut and paste text blocks from one program to another. DOS packages are generally limited to moving blocks within a document, or at least among documents originating in the same program. However, word processing programs that run under Windows offer the same cut-and-paste capabilities found on the Macintosh. Another distinction is the amount of text that can be cut or copied at the same time. WordStar, for example, lets you cut and paste relatively large blocks of text, but if the block is too large you won't be able to undo the operation later.

Search-and-replace allows you to replace every occurrence of a certain word with another word. For example, you can replace all "Volkswagens" in an article with "Corvettes." The search-and-replace functions in different word processors vary in the degree of flexibility they provide. Some allow you to perform wild-card searches. For example, you can look for every four-letter word that begins "WOR." Some packages allow you to find and replace text styles and hidden characters that control line breaks and other formatting. This can save a lot of time if you need to convert a document from one format to another.

One factor that affects editing productivity is the ease of getting around a document. Most packages have commands that move you automatically to the beginning or end of a file, or to a particular page. Some allow you to place markers in a document that you can jump to with a quick command.

Macintosh and Windows packages again have an advantage when it comes to moving through a document file. With a mouse, you can quickly position the cursor at any screen location where editing must be performed. In addition, most Macintosh and Windows programs use a common "scroll bar" on the side of the screen to provide an intuitive method for moving through a file. This is a small, shaded bar with arrows at each end and a small box that can be moved up and down. The box's position in the bar indicates your location in the document. If it is in the middle of the bar, for example, you are halfway through the file. Click once on one of the arrows and the document moves up or down one line at a time. Click on the bar above or below the box and the page scrolls one screen at a time. To move quickly from one end of the document to the other, you simply drag the box to the appropriate location on the bar.

Windowing features are yet another advantage of word

Windowing functions allow you to display multiple views of one or more files simultaneously on one screen.

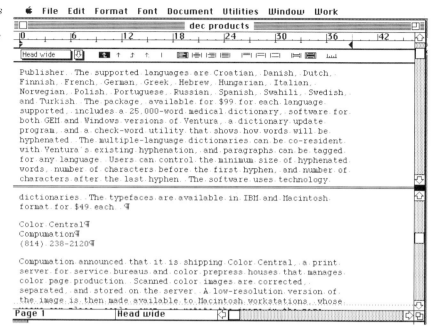

processing programs that run under a graphical interface. These functions allow you to display multiple views of one or more files simultaneously on one screen. For example, if your word processor permits it, a window in the upper half of your screen might display a file about automobile manufacturers, while a window on the bottom displays car makes and models. You can then scroll through each file, cutting and pasting text from one to the other.

Most DOS-based word processing packages include some sort of windowing function, but they tend to be limited in the number of views they can display. The Macintosh includes windowing as a built-in feature of its system software. With some Macintosh packages, your ability to open multiple windows is limited only by your computer's memory. All Macintosh word processors use the same procedures for opening, closing, and resizing windows.

Formatting

As with editing features, formatting functions are essential ingredients in the typical word processing package. These include features that allow you to set margins, indents, tabs, multiple columns, page breaks, and other layout-oriented functions. They also include features that allow you to select text attributes like typeface, font size and alignment. Some packages offer style sheet functions that allow you to automate the process of formatting text.

All word processing packages allow you to set margins, tabs, indents, and the like. Where they differ is in their method for doing so. With some packages, you must enter numeric measurements indicating where margins or tabs should be set. Others, especially those on the Macintosh, allow you to set margins by adjusting a ruler line that appears at the top of the document. The best packages give you the option of doing both. Though it is generally easier to set a margin by visual means, numeric measurements allow for greater precision.

One area where word processing packages differ is in how they handle pagination. Most programs use what's known as background pagination. This means you can see where page breaks fall in a document as you enter or edit text. Page-oriented word processors that view documents as a compilation of pages require that you enter a specific command to show page breaks.

Another area where word processors vary is in their ability to produce and display multiple-column layouts. Most packages can produce a two- or three-column layout, but there are vast differences in their ability to display the multiple columns. The DOS version of Word, for example, offers three display modes. In draft mode, you can enter text to be formatted into multiple columns, but you do not see this formatting. In layout mode, you can see the columns side-by-side on the screen as you edit them, but you cannot see graphic images. In preview mode, you can see a realistic representation of the page, complete with graphics, but you cannot make any edits. WordStar, on the other hand, is limited to two views: draft and preview. Instead of displaying columns side-by-side, WordStar uses symbol characters in the left-most column of the screen to indicate which column a particular section of text is in. A symbol with one line means the text is in column one, two lines indicates column two, and so on.

Other formatting features include headers and footers. Headers are lines of type that appear at the top of every page or every alternating page. Footers are lines that appear at the bottom. Most packages provide the ability to specify a header or footer for all pages. Some offer the added flexibility of providing separate headers and footers for odd- and even-numbered pages, while others allow you to vary or delete the header or footer on a particular page. Another variable is whether the package allows you to include a graphic image in the header or footer.

The most powerful word processors include an especially useful feature known as style sheets. A style sheet is essentially a list of formatting instructions. It generally consists of "tags" or "styles" that contain a complete set of formatting commands for a line or paragraph of text. For example, a style sheet might include a "headline" tag that defines headlines as being in 14-point Helvetica bold aligned in the center of the page with a half inch of space above and a quarter inch below. When you use the style sheet with a particular document, you can then "tag" a line of text with the headline style to have it automatically assume the defined characteristics. In addition to allowing quick text formatting, style sheets make it easy to change the entire look of a document. If you decide, for example, that you want headlines in 18-point Times instead of 14-point Helvetica, you merely change the appropriate tag and the headlines are automatically transformed.

Writing Aids

Beyond basic editing and formatting features are extra functions that make a writer's life easier: spell-checking and the on-line thesaurus. A spell checker allows you to search through a document for misspelled words, automatically correcting them at your request. Almost all word processing packages include this capability, though the actual quality of spell-checking functions varies from package to package.

The typical spell checker includes a default dictionary containing common words. In addition, you can usually add your own words or create your own custom user dictionaries to supplement the default word list. Typically, these extra dictionaries are created as you perform a spell check. When the program flags a "misspelled" word that should be included in the dictionary, you merely issue a command to do so. Some spell checkers will flag repeated occurrences of an unknown word even if the user has indicated that the word is not misspelled. The better ones will skip subsequent occurrences.

It would seem logical that a big spelling dictionary is better than a small one. But in reality, a large dictionary can be a disadvantage if it contains a lot of obscure words that have similar spellings to common ones. For example, a dictionary with a lot of medical terms might ignore the word "quittor," since that is the term for a horse disease in addition to being a potential misspelling of "quitter."

A function related to spell-checking is the on-line thesaurus, which quickly locates synonyms for words highlighted by the user. In practical terms, this is less useful than spell-checking because of the general limitations in conventional thesauruses. This has to do with the requirements for good writing: if a word is so obscure that you can only find it in a thesaurus, you are probably better off not using it anyway. Still, some users like being able to search for synonyms. Many developers of word processing packages, rather than develop their own electronic thesauruses, use products created by third parties. One of the most popular of these is WordFinder from Microlytics, which is used by WordStar and Microsoft Word.

One area where thesauruses differ is the kinds of linkages they allow. The simpler ones will merely display a list of synonyms for a particular word. Better thesauruses provide links to further synonyms for each word in the original list.

Document Management

"Document management" features are aimed at easing the production of lengthy documents, especially books and technical or academic reports. Because they are most useful for relatively complex documents, these features often define the difference between professional-level packages and managerial ones. They include such functions as indexing, table-of-contents generation, footnotes, and cross-references.

Indexing functions generally allow you to produce a standard one- or two-level index. With most packages, the user does this by entering codes in a document file next to words that should be indexed. Others allow you to create an "index list" of words to appear in the index; the program then searches the document for words on the list, building the index accordingly. Either method vastly simplifies an otherwise laborious task.

Outlining functions allow you to define your document as a multi-level outline, and are especially helpful for organizing complex documents. Suppose you are writing a guide to motor vehicle laws in each state. You have six main headings for each region in the nation—Northeast, Southeast, Midwest, Southwest, Rocky Mountain States, and Pacific—then subheadings for each state within the region. An outlining function allows you to define the regional sections as level one headlines and the state sections as level two headlines. You could then collapse the document so that you can see just level one headlines, just level two headlines, both sets of headlines, or all text.

Some word processing packages include built-in outlining

functions. You can define a document as an outline without leaving the main application. Other packages provide outlining as a function that must be run separately.

One function related to outlining and indexing is table-of-contents generation. With this feature, you can define headings and sub-headings in your document as table-of-contents entries. The program then searches the document for headings to create a multi-level table of contents. Some professional-level programs also allow you to create separate tables of illustrations or other items that appear throughout a document.

Cross-referencing is an especially useful function in documents with tables or illustrations. Although the functions are implemented differently in different programs, they generally allow you to insert references to other sections of a document when you are not sure just where those sections will fall. For example, you can refer to a table that appears on page "x," inserting a code that links that reference to the actual table. When the document is printed, the program determines on which page the table will appear, and inserts the appropriate number in the reference.

Footnoting features allow you to attach a footnote to a reference in the body of text. The user typically issues a footnote command at the point in text where the footnoted comment appears. A bibliographic reference or annotation can then be entered into a pop-up window that appears. When the document is printed, properly numbered footnotes appear at the bottom of the page or end of the chapter.

Redlining is a useful feature in environments where multiple authors or editors participate in document production. It allows a user to suggest revisions to a text file without actually making them. In Microsoft Word's redlining mode, for example, text that would normally be deleted is instead struck through with a horizontal line, while inserted text is underlined. At the user's option, a vertical bar can be printed in the margin to indicate that the paragraph has been revised. The author can then search for revised text and issue commands to accept or reject suggested changes.

Graphics

Another area where professional-level word processing packages distinguish themselves is graphics. More and more, word processing programs are adding the ability to import and display graphic images. Some even provide limited tools for resizing or cropping (cutting away part of) pictures. However, even the high-end packages are generally weak in their graphics-handling capabilities when compared with most desktop publishing programs.

On the DOS side, packages that include graphics import capability are limited in their ability to display the images. In most cases, the program will display a shaded box or line indicating that an image has been inserted. To actually view the image, you must print it or use a print preview function. However, Windows-based word processing programs like Ami Professional or Word for Windows can present a WYSIWYG view of the page that rivals the capabilities of most publishing programs.

Macintosh word processors can display graphics as they are imported, but the programs are still limited in their ability to handle images. In most cases, images are treated as if they are characters that have been entered at the keyboard. To move the image to the right, you place the cursor next to it and hit the space bar. To move it down, you hit the Return key. Publishing programs, on the other hand, allow you to move images by dragging them with the mouse.

Another general limitation among word processors, at least on the DOS side, is the range of graphics file formats they support. Several graphics formats, such as PCX and TIFF, have become near-standards because of their association with certain graphics or publishing programs. While some word processing packages (notably Word and WordPerfect) support these common formats, others do not. Instead, you must convert the images into the word processing program's graphic format using a utility program.

Printing Features

A word processor with the best editing and formatting features ever seen would still not be worth very much if it couldn't produce a printed page. Almost all word processing packages allow you to produce hard copy on a wide range of output devices, including dot-matrix and laser printers. Where they differ is in the range of devices supported and the degree to which they take full advantage of a printer's features.

With the emergence of laser printers, most word processors have added extensive features that allow you to select fonts and insert high-resolution graphic images. Most include support for PostScript printers; almost all will print on Hewlett-Packard's LaserJet. If the program runs on the Macintosh or under Windows, printing functions are generally handled by the

When using the mail-merge function, you set up a letter with codes in place of the recipient's name and address. The program inserts names and addresses from a data file, producing a personalized form letter for each person on your mailing list.

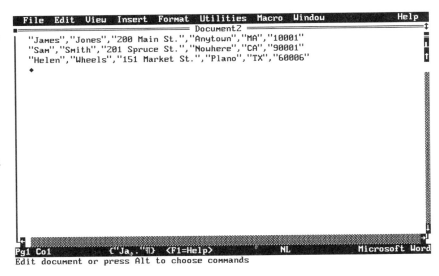

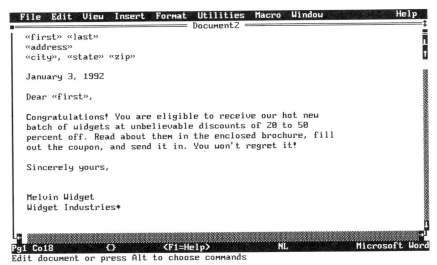

system software. DOS programs, however, include their own printing routines.

The ability to produce pages that combine graphics and typographic-quality fonts has created a need for a way to preview that output. Most word processors include a graphical preview function that lets you see on-screen a more-or-less accurate representation of how the finished page will look. Some programs provide little more than thumbnail sketches that show a reduced view of the page. Others, such as the WordStar page preview, allow you to zoom in to read magnified portions of a page.

Background printing is a helpful feature no matter what kind of printer you use. It allows you to edit a document or perform other tasks as the program prints your document. Some packages that allow background printing exact a performance penalty (depending in part on the hardware): the program responds slowly to the user's input as the page is being printed. Other packages show little hint that a document is being printed. Macintosh word processors running under Apple's Multifinder operating system provide background printing as an automatic feature.

One feature found almost universally in word processing packages is mail-merge (or merge-print), which allows you to produce personalized form letters. These functions work by combining information from two files: a document file containing the letter, and a data file containing the names, addresses, and other information on the addressees. The data file is typically in a standard format like ASCII, a "United Nations" of text file formats that is supported by almost all software packages. When you compose the letter, you specify the name of the data file and enter codes in place of variable information like the recipient's name and address. The program produces letters for each record in the data file, inserting names, addresses, and other information as specified by the user.

Some mail-merge functions allow you to vary what's printed in the letters depending on the information in the data files. For example, you can set up your system so that certain paragraphs are printed in letters going to Texas, while other paragraphs are printed in letters going elsewhere. A few packages are sold with optional file management programs that allow you to keep data files for use with the merge-print function. However, almost all file or database management programs can produce data files for mail-merge applications.

Extras

Beyond the features that are more-or-less essential for producing various kinds of documents, many word processors include functions that would not obviously appear to belong in an editorial package. Some users will find, however, that these features often come in handy in the course of producing certain kinds of documents.

Almost all DOS packages include the ability to run DOS commands without leaving the program. This means you can quickly copy or delete files or even run other programs, if your computer's memory permits it. This latter capability is helpful if you must move frequently between your word processor and a database or spreadsheet package.

Most packages also include a math function that allows you to perform simple calculations. Typically, the user highlights a section of text containing a mathematical equation, then issues a command to perform the calculation. Sorting functions allow you to highlight a list of words that are then sorted into alphabetical order.

Some packages include built-in telecommunications software. This allows users equipped with a modem to dial up on-line information services like Compuserve, through which you can read the latest headlines and stock quotes, order airline tickets, or engage in a transcontinental dialog with other computer users. You can also call into computer bulletin boards and exchange information with other modem-equipped computers. Some vendors of word processing packages offer their own bulletin boards or Compuserve user forums.

Macintosh Packages

Microsoft Word

Microsoft Word remains the market leader among Macintosh-based word processors. It is a comprehensive editorial tool, offering strong indexing, outlining, and spell-check functions. Because it takes advantage of the Macintosh user interface, it is also easy to use considering its wide range of features. It works especially well in conjunction with Macintosh-based page-makeup programs like Aldus PageMaker and QuarkXPress.

Word has one of the best style-sheet functions on the market. You can assign variables like typeface, type size, line spacing and others to styles that can be assigned to sections of text. These styles can be grouped so that they occur in any desired sequence within the document. For example, you can have a headline tag that is always followed by a body text tag. Another strength of Word's style sheet function is that it is directly supported by PageMaker and QuarkXPress. When a Word document is imported into the page-makeup program, so are any styles applied within the word processing software. Word also includes a flexible table-editing feature that makes it easy to insert and edit tabular material. However, the tables cannot be directly imported into a page-makeup program. Instead,

Microsoft Word is the market leader among Macintosh-based word processors.

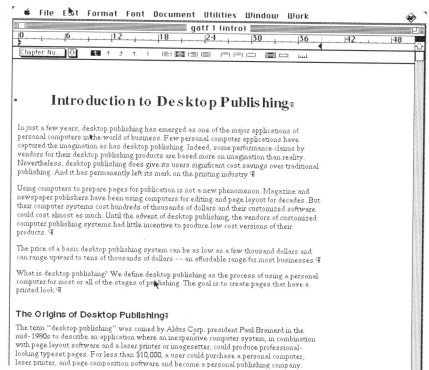

they must be converted into a format in which columns are separated by tab stops.

Other useful features include a "smart quotes" option that allows you to enter correctly curved quotation marks without resorting to arcane command-key combinations, and a word count function that displays the number of characters, words, lines, or paragraphs in a selected section of text or the entire document. A customization function allows you to add or delete any program command to or from any desired menu. As you add a command to a menu, you can also assign a keystroke combination that allows you to invoke the command from the keyboard. These custom menu structures can be saved and loaded, allowing you to set up various formats for different kinds of documents.

WordPerfect

WordPerfect, one of the leading word processing programs for DOS computers, is also available in a Macintosh version. The original Macintosh version, released in 1989, failed to make effective use of the graphical interface and was generally panned by Macintosh users. However, version 2.0, released in

1991, does a much better job of integrating the program's powerful functions into the Macintosh environment.

Like Word, WordPerfect offers a powerful style sheet function. But its revision control and macro capabilities exceed Word's. Text can easily be marked for insertion or deletion, and revisions can be quickly undone. The macro function allows creation of simple programs that automate various aspects of using WordPerfect. Unlike the macro functions in other word processors, WordPerfect's macros can include loops, memory variables, and subroutines; can prompt the user for input; and can even be debugged using a function that goes through the macro line-by-line. WordPerfect also includes drawing tools that can be used to create simple diagrams and illustrations, even in color.

Nisus

Nisus is a powerful Macintosh word processor from a small developer called Paragon Concepts in Del Mar, CA. Though it takes longer to master than other Macintosh word processors, it boasts many unique features and has the most powerful search-and-replace function of any major word processor on the market.

Like most word processors, Nisus can search for occurrences

Nisus, a word processing package for the Macintosh, includes a powerful search-and-replace function.

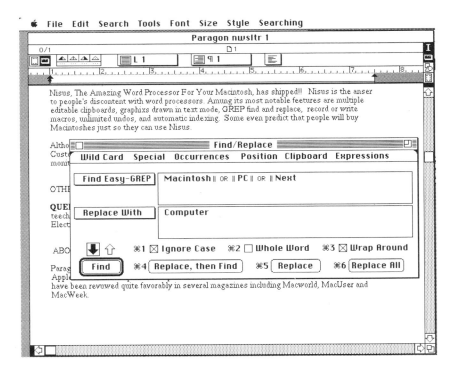

of one word and replace them with another. But it goes far beyond this by including a pattern-matching function called GREP, for Global Recognition Expression Parser. GREP is a mini-programming language that allows you to construct complex search patterns that use wild card characters and variables. For example, you can search for all phone numbers in the 999-999-9999 format and change them to (999) 999-9999. Or you can search for duplicate words, such as "the the," and delete one of them.

The macro facility is also powerful, especially when used in conjunction with GREP. Macros can include Nisus commands, memory variables, and calls to open a Macintosh desk accessory. Macros can also include other macros (even themselves). Just about any operation that can be performed with Nisus can be programmed into a macro. One macro included with the program provides its mail-merge capability, attesting to the power of the macro language.

Nisus also includes functions for drawing, cross-referencing, spell-checking, and generating an index or table of contents. Its undo function allows you to undo nearly every operation up to when the document was last saved. A statistics box lists the number of words and paragraphs along with a "readability score."

Despite this power, Nisus is not for everybody. The GREP language requires some programming expertise if you want to perform complex search-and-replace operations. Table-generating functions are weak, and its style sheet feature is not quite as powerful as Word's.

MacWrite II

MacWrite II, a descendant of the original Macintosh word processor, is sold by Apple subsidiary Claris Corp. It falls squarely into the "managerial" category, lacking some of the more advanced features in Word and WordPerfect, but making up for this with its ease of use. Though it is not as powerful as the professional-level packages, it is well suited for producing many kinds of documents and also works well as a text entry tool for documents that will eventually be formatted in a page-makeup program.

MacWrite's mail-merge function is relatively powerful, with the ability to alter the content of form letters depending on the information in the merged database. The program's style sheet feature is rather limited: you can save type characteristics (font, size, etc.) as a style, but not paragraph settings (alignment, line spacing, etc.). However, you can automatically apply the format of one paragraph to another, and the program's search-and-replace function allows you to change typefaces and sizes in addition to character strings.

WriteNow

T/Maker's WriteNow is another popular Macintosh word processor that falls into the managerial category. It lacks many of the professional-level features found in Microsoft Word or WordPerfect, but is well-suited for simple office documents like correspondence, memos, and reports. It also works well as a front-end for desktop publishing.

WriteNow includes most of the features that have become basic requirements in word processing programs in its price range. These include search-and-replace, a customizable spell checker, and mail merge. A smart-quote feature automatically converts quotation marks to the appropriate right- or left-curled format. You can also insert the date, time, and other data by means of insertion commands in the Edit menu. However, WriteNow lacks such professional-level features as outlining, cross-references, and index or table-of-contents generation.

DOS-Based Packages

Most word processors on the PC retain the traditional text-based display, though with a few wrinkles. Words are still entered, edited, and formatted in the familiar 80-column-by-24-line display, but most packages also offer a preview mode that lets you see a representation of the page before it's printed. Another common feature in the newer packages is support for laser printers, including PostScript-based devices. The two leaders in the DOS word processing market are WordPerfect and Microsoft Word. Other leading packages include WordStar and Signature (formerly known as XyWrite).

WordPerfect

WordPerfect has been the top-selling word processor for PC environments during the last several years. Today, it is well established as a full-featured word processor that offers a dazzling array of text manipulation, formatting, and graphic capabilities. The package offers complete support for laser printers and on-screen document preview, including display of integrated charts and other graphics. With the proper graphics display hardware, WordPerfect will also show proportional fonts on screen exactly as they will print.

WordPerfect has a powerful mail merge capability that can insert different paragraphs at print time depending on information in the data file. Outlining capabilities are also strong. For column work, WordPerfect will support up to 24 snaking or parallel columns on a page. Its undo command allows up to three sets of deleted material to be recovered.

On the downside, WordPerfect offers a bewildering variety of keystroke combinations to control all its capabilities. The commands are not all that intuitive, and many users find that they must simply memorize the keystrokes they use most often and refer to the documentation or keyboard "cheat sheets" for others. However, the on-line documentation offers an interactive tutorial, context-sensitive help, and complete explanations of most user options.

WordPerfect compensates for some of its complexity by means of a sophisticated macro system that allows you to perform a complex operation just once and then have the program replay the same keystrokes on its own. However, with so many command keystrokes already built into the program, you may be hard-pressed to find open key combinations to designate as macros.

Microsoft Word

Microsoft Word is WordPerfect's major competitor in the DOS word processing market. The program's advantages include speedy performance, a comprehensive feature set, and a well-designed user interface that provides easy access to most of its major functions. In addition to the usual mail-merge, outline, spell-check, index, and windowing functions, it includes powerful features for handling graphics, tables, macros, cross-references, and style sheets. Style sheets, for example, can apply attributes like paragraph spacing and line break effects, in addition to typeface, size, and style, to selected sections of text. You can create formats for common documents, then store them for later use. Glossaries can be used to store keyboard macros containing commonly used text or commands.

Graphics can be inserted in a wide variety of formats, including Lotus PIC (for graphs), and PostScript. Files in TIFF and PCX formats can also be imported. You can resize and position graphics with a lot of accuracy, but not as easily as you can with a desktop publishing package. A "hot links" feature allows users to link tables created in Word with the spreadsheet program that generates the data. Tables are automatically updated as information is added to the original spreadsheet file.

Another strength in Word is its user interface. The original version of the program featured a spreadsheet-like interface in which the user hit the Escape key to access menu options at the bottom of the screen. Version 5.5, introduced in 1990, introduced a visual (but still character-based) interface featuring pull-down menus and a scroll bar. Frequently used features can also be accessed by means of function keys. This approach makes the program easy to learn (considering its complexity), but also highly productive once you get the hang of it. The package is not as easy to use as the Macintosh or Windows versions (which have the advantage of a graphical interface), but the developers have done a good job of working within the limitations of a text-based interface.

WordStar

WordStar, first developed for the old CP/M environment, was one of the first business-oriented word processing programs for microcomputers. As a result, many users grew accustomed to its complex series of dot commands and key combinations for controlling basic functions. The PC version, which retained the basic approach of the CP/M version, was quickly overtaken by programs like Word and WordPerfect that took advantage of the PC's function keys and its relatively powerful hardware. However, the program retained a loyal following among many users, and its developer (originally known as MicroPro and now known as WordStar International) has steadily upgraded its capabilities.

In its present form, WordStar offers a choice of two interfaces. Experienced users (and touch typists) can employ the traditional control-key combinations, which some find to be faster than menu-based approaches. But WordStar also has a set of optional pull-down menus that provide access to its functions for less experienced users.

After a steady stream of upgrades, WordStar now offers a feature set that competes with the leaders of the DOS word processing market. Functions added to the later versions include style sheets, extensive laser printer support, and a powerful page preview function. It is also highly customizable thanks to an easy-to-use utility program included with the package.

Signature

Signature, from XyQuest, has a rather interesting history. It originated in a program called XyWrite that was one of the early word processors for PC-compatible computers. XyWrite was characterized by a rather difficult interface that required users to enter commands to access functions. However, it was also fast and highly modifiable, allowing creation of custom menus and macros for access to commands. Editorial departments of magazines or other publications could hire a programmer to customize the package for use by their writers and editors, complete with extensive (and unique) menu structures. A few software developers even used XyWrite as the basis for their own word processing products.

IBM, looking to shore up its microcomputer software offerings, acquired marketing and distribution rights to XyWrite in 1990 and changed the name to Signature. Working under contract to IBM, XyQuest also revamped the package, adding pull-down menus, graphical preview capabilities, and a host of other new features. However, shortly before the program was to be released, IBM closed its desktop software unit and XyQuest reassumed marketing and distribution responsibilities.

The program that emerged from all this is a powerful one, with features that rival those in Word and WordPerfect. Though it uses a character-based interface, it also includes a graphic view mode that shows the page pretty much as it will be printed. However, unlike the preview modes in other character-based word processors, Signature allows users to edit most of the text in the graphic view (the exceptions are headers, footers, and footnotes). Signature also offers a document management function that displays useful information about each text file. It automatically records the name of the original author, the last person to edit the document, and the number of revisions made to the document (the number is increased each time changes are made and the file is closed).

Though most users will access features through the Signature menus, the program also retains its command interface as an option. These commands can be used as part of the Signature Programming Language to automate software operations and customize the package, much as you could with the original XyWrite.

Windows Packages

The hottest new trend on the PC side is the graphical word processor. These programs, most of which run under Microsoft Windows, provide a WYSIWYG layout mode and other Macintosh-like features. Some come pretty close to desktop publishing functionality. However, because they run under Windows, they are not suitable for use on older XT- or AT-type computers.

Some of these programs straddle the boundary between word processing and desktop publishing by offering two modes: a draft mode designed for quick text entry and editing, and a layout mode for page composition functions. You don't have quite as many formatting options as you'd find in a desktop publishing program, but they are more than sufficient for the typical word processing user.

Ami Professional

Ami Professional, one of the first Windows-based word processors, was developed by a company called Samna Corp. In 1990, Samna was acquired by Lotus Development, which assumed responsibility for maintaining and marketing the product. Samna originally offered two versions of the program: Ami, which was positioned as a relatively simple managerial-level word processor, and Ami Professional, which includes nearly every document production feature the developers could dream of. Lotus now offers Ami under the name "Lotus Write."

Ami Professional is a word processing program with page layout features that rival those of page-makeup packages like Aldus PageMaker and Ventura Publisher. Its style sheet feature is similar to Ventura's, allowing users to create style tags that define the typeface, type size, paragraph spacing, and other formatting characteristics. Its graphics functions are also reminiscent of the desktop publishing approach. You can draw a frame on the screen and import graphic images in PCX, TIFF, and EPS formats. Graphics can be cropped, resized, or rotated. An image processing dialog box allows you to adjust various settings for photographic images. The program also includes a built-in drawing program with which you can create images consisting of lines, boxes, and circles. A charting function allows users to import spreadsheet data, which is automatically converted into one of several types of graphs. Its table editor makes it easy to create complex tables.

Despite this power, Ami Professional has a well conceived user interface that makes the program relatively easy to learn and operate. The program offers a draft mode for quick text entry and a layout mode for page composition. Most functions can be accessed through menu selections or by clicking on icons in a toolbox on the side of the screen. A customization feature allows users to add the most frequently used functions to the toolbox.

Word for Windows

Microsoft's Word for Windows has much in common with the Macintosh version of Word. However, its approach to document production also bears some resemblance to Ami's. Like Ami, it offers a choice between a draft mode for quick entry of text and a layout mode that allows you to see fonts, graphics, and other page elements pretty much as they'll be printed.

Word for Windows provides many of its formatting features by means of a ruler bar that appears at the top of the screen. You can also choose to have a "ribbon" bar appear, which provides access to font and type size selections. The style sheet feature is every bit as strong as those in the other versions of Word. A glossary function allows storage of frequently used text or graphics that can be quickly called into a document. With the program's macro feature, you can assign any command or series of commands to a key or menu. The spell-check function is especially powerful, offering the ability to check spelling in multiple languages within the same document. Document templates, which can include constant text, style sheets, glossary items, and macros, can be saved and reused in other documents.

Other features include a table editor (similar to the one in the Macintosh version), mathematical equation editor, a powerful outlining function, indexing, footnotes, table of contents generation, and the ability to add hidden comments. The program also includes a built-in grammar checker and charting and drawing functions.

WordStar for Windows

WordStar for Windows, introduced in 1991, is derived from NBI's Legacy, a Windows program (described in the next chapter) that combines word processing and page-makeup functions. Like Word for Windows and Ami Professional, it offers a draft mode for quick text entry and a layout mode for page composition. The program handles graphics in much the same manner as a page layout program: the user draws a frame on the page, into which the image is imported. The program also includes a table editor, cross-references, style sheets, drawing tools, and a thesaurus that includes synonyms, antonyms, near synonyms and antonyms, and word definitions. Its typographic controls rival those in many page-makeup programs, providing control of leading, kerning, and tracking to 1/1000th of an em.

The programs described here are by no means the only word processing packages suitable for use in a desktop publishing system. Dozens of vendors offer word processing programs for a wide range of computers, each with their own strengths and weaknesses. Some of these programs are directly supported by page-makeup software, while others can produce ASCII text files that can be imported into PageMaker, QuarkXPress, Ventura Publisher, and other programs.

Now that we have covered the text entry process, we're ready to take a look at page layout. We do this in the next chapter, on desktop publishing software.

Chapter Four

Desktop Publishing Programs

For most users, desktop publishing packages are the principal means of producing publications. These programs, also known as page layout or page composition packages, allow users to create a wide range of publications using desktop computers. Typically, the user is shown an on-screen representation of a page layout on which text and graphics can be positioned. Most desktop publishing programs have limited tools for creating text and graphics. Instead, they are designed to incorporate text and graphics created with other programs.

Desktop publishing programs vary widely in their functions and capabilities. Low-end packages are suited mostly for producing flyers and other simple one-page documents. More complex publishing packages include sophisticated features like style sheets, indexing, and typographic functions that offer precise control over character spacing. Some word processing packages have page layout and graphics import features that approach the functionality of desktop publishing software. At the same time, many desktop publishing programs are adding features like spell checking and find-and-replace that were once the province of word processing packages.

In this chapter, we'll look at several leading desktop publishing programs to see how their features compare.

Macintosh Programs

Aldus PageMaker
Aldus PageMaker has long occupied a leading position among desktop publishing packages for the Macintosh. Competing programs, such as QuarkXPress, Ventura Publisher, and FrameMaker, may have more to offer in several key areas, but PageMaker remains a viable option for users who need a good

*One of
PageMaker's major
strengths is its
highly intuitive
user interface*

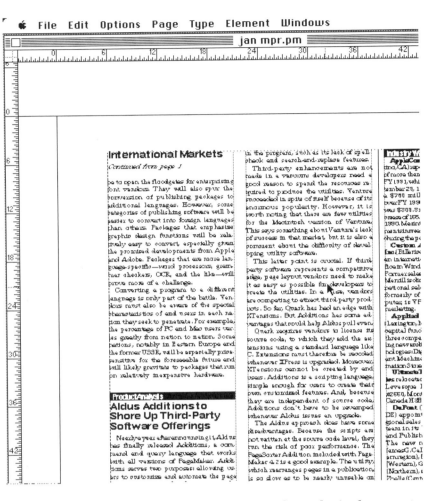

general-purpose publishing tool that is also relatively easy to use.

One of PageMaker's major strengths is its highly intuitive user interface. When you launch the program, you are presented with an electronic version of a pasteup board. A "Place" command allows you to import text and graphics in a wide variety of formats. These elements can be positioned on the page or moved to the side for use elsewhere in the publication. An on-screen toolbox includes functions for entering text, cropping graphics, and adding rules, ellipses, and boxes.

PageMaker's productivity is much enhanced by a style sheet function. The user can create style tags that include settings for typeface, type size, type style, paragraph spacing, and other variables. To apply the style to a paragraph, the user places the cursor anywhere within and clicks on the tag name in a style palette that appears on the screen.

The program's color functions allow users to apply spot colors to any element on the page, employing either the Pantone system or mixtures of process colors. If you use the former, you can produce spot color overlays directly from PageMaker. To produce CYMK separations of spot colors or photographs, you must use a separate program called Aldus PrePrint.

PageMaker has traditionally been best suited to producing relatively short documents, such as brochures, newsletters, and flyers. However, early versions were less useful for producing long documents, such as books and reports, that have a consistent format. Newer versions of the program have added numerous functions that address this weakness. One is an indexing feature that automatically creates indices with up to three levels. A Book feature allows you to combine multiple chapters into a single publication. The style sheet function has also been enhanced. You can create tags that automatically add rules above or below a paragraph. A "Keep with next" setting prevents page or column breaks between two specified paragraphs.

Other useful features include the Story Editor, a built-in word processor that makes it much easier to enter text from scratch. Though you would not want to write an entire book with the Story Editor, you can enter large blocks of text and have them quickly placed on the page. Along with the Story Editor, PageMaker includes spell check and search-and-replace functions that are similar to what you might find in a word processor. Another feature allows you to build links between the PageMaker document and constituent files created with word processing programs. Once you create a link, any changes made in PageMaker are reflected in the original file. A separate Table Editor allows you to create tables that are then exported to PageMaker in the Macintosh PICT format.

PageMaker also includes several typographic functions that can be helpful in improving the appearance of type. A tracking feature allows you to apply five levels of tracking, from very loose to very tight, to paragraphs. A text rotation function allows you to rotate text in 90-degree increments. Type can also be expanded or condensed.

With the release of PageMaker 4.2 early in 1992, Aldus introduced a new technology called Additions that allows users to automate various aspects of using the program. Additions is a scripting language that allows users to store PageMaker commands in a macro file. The Additions technology is also used by software developers to create add-on utility products for PageMaker.

QuarkXPress

QuarkXPress has long been a favorite of publishers and designers who need a sophisticated page layout tool for the Macintosh. It offers powerful functions for handling type, graphics, and other elements of the page composition process. The developers have also improved the program's user interface, making it nearly as friendly as its rival, Aldus PageMaker, despite the wide range of features.

XPress uses text and graphics "boxes" as the basic elements of the page layout. It also features a "pasteboard" metaphor reminiscent of PageMaker. You can drag items from the page to the pasteboard, but you cannot move them to other pages as you can with the Aldus product. A powerful "Library" option allows you to store frequently used text and graphic elements, which can be easily pasted into the document. A Document Layout palette presents a thumbnail view of the pages within the document. Pages can be easily rearranged by dragging the thumbnails with the mouse. Each document can include up to 127 master pages, which contain recurring text and graphics elements.

QuarkXPress does not include a built-in text editor, but it

QuarkXPress uses text and graphics "boxes" as the basic elements of the page layout.

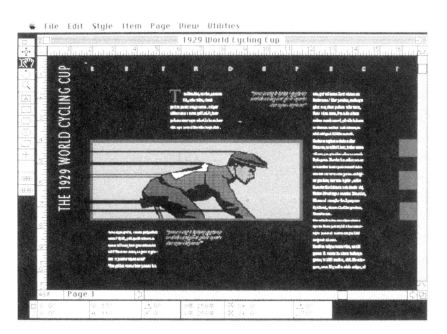

does offer search-and-replace and spell-check functions. The program's style sheet function is powerful, with widow and orphan control and the ability to keep lines and paragraphs together. Other key features include automatic drop caps, vertical justification, and the ability to rotate text in one-degree increments.

In addition to its sophisticated typographic features, QuarkXPress is also known for its extensive graphics functions. You can select multiple elements, and align or group them. You can choose from several Picture Box shapes, including round, square, or polygonal, or create your own. Images can be rotated in one-degree increments or slanted. You can also enlarge or reduce images in increments of 0.1 percent. Almost all of the popular Macintosh paint and draw formats are supported.

The program's color printing functions are among the best of any Macintosh page layout program. You can apply Pantone or process colors to text and graphic elements, and produce spot color separations directly from the program. To produce separations of color TIFF files, you need a companion program called SpectreSeps QX. New is the ability to create traps, a technique that corrects for poor registration of spot color separations.

QuarkXPress uses a limited form of copy protection: it automatically checks for copies of the same program running on an AppleTalk network. The program runs on a Macintosh SE, but a more powerful Macintosh II series computer is recommended for adequate performance.

Ready,Set,Go

Ready,Set,Go was one of the early entrants in the Macintosh desktop publishing market. Originally developed by a company called Manhattan Graphics, it was acquired by Letraset in 1987. It enjoyed a reasonably high volume of sales for a few years, but Letraset was slow to upgrade the product, and before long competing packages like PageMaker and QuarkXPress far surpassed its capabilities with a series of upgrades. In response to this, Letraset reduced the list price for the program by 50 percent and positioned it as an entry-level application.

Letraset released a more sophisticated version of the package called DesignStudio in 1990 (see below), but it also failed to make an impression in the market. In 1991, Manhattan Graphics reacquired the rights to both Ready,Set,Go and DesignStudio and is now responsible for developing, marketing, and distributing the software.

Ready,Set,Go builds pages using text and picture blocks. To

place text, for example, you draw a text block on the page and select a file for import. Supported text formats include Microsoft Word, MacWrite, and ASCII. Text can also be exported in ASCII format. The program retains the word processor's formatting, such as boldface and italics, but cannot read style sheet information. However, it does include a simple style sheet function. Text and paragraph formats can be saved as styles, which can then be applied elsewhere in the document. However, the function lacks some formatting options found in competing programs, such as the ability to include rules as part of the style.

The program's major strength is in its typographic features. It supports kerning and tracking, and allows selection of type sizes in increments of 0.01 points. It does not use a hyphenation dictionary, but the algorithm used to separate words generally works well. Lacking, however, are vertical justification and widow and orphan control.

Another strength is found in some of the text editing features. The program was one of the first to include a spell checker and search-and-replace function. You can also define keyboard macros that automate certain aspects of the program's operation. Missing, however, are long document features like indexing, auto-numbering, and table-of-contents generation.

Ready,Set,Go can import graphics in MacPaint, PICT, EPSF, and TIFF formats. Once an image is imported, it can be cropped or scaled. You can also perform simple image-editing operations on scanned photographs. The program can produce spot color overlays, but cannot handle process color.

DesignStudio

DesignStudio could be renamed "Ready,Set,Go Plus." It bears some resemblance to its low-priced sibling, but goes much further in offering sophisticated page composition and production features.

The program's basic approach to page layout is similar to Ready,Set,Go's. Text and graphics are imported by means of text and picture blocks placed on the page. However, the program offers some options not found in any other page layout program. For example, you can place text inside one of 15 odd shapes, such as a triangle. Text and graphic blocks can also be rotated in one-degree increments.

DesignStudio includes a powerful style sheet function for storage of text and paragraph formatting options. You can apply a certain set of formatting options to a block of text, then store them as a style, or build the style directly by entering formatting commands. Styles can also be imported from Macintosh word processors, such as Microsoft Word.

Typographic features are also impressive. A kerning option allows you to determine the spacing between any two characters in a particular font. The kerned characters are shown in a preview box, allowing for quick corrections to any settings you've entered. You can also copy kerning information from one font to another. A tracking function allows for global adjustment of character spacing within a particular font. The hyphenation function uses a preset algorithm, but you can also define your own word breaks that are stored in an exception dictionary.

With Letraset's emphasis on graphics applications, it should not be surprising that DesignStudio includes extensive features for creating and modifying graphics. In addition to the standard tools for drawing lines, boxes, and circles, the program allows for creation of user-definable arrowheads.

One nice aspect of DesignStudio is that it treats all text and graphics as objects that can be permanently grouped. For example, you can group a graphic image with a block of text. Whenever you move the text, the graphic moves with it. Objects can also be stored in a library for later use in other documents.

Color output features are also impressive. You can apply spot or process colors to text and graphic elements, and you can also import color graphics in TIFF, RIFF, PICT, and PostScript formats. Color separations can be produced with DesignStudio Separator, a utility program included free with the package. The Separator program is compatible with Letraset's ColorStudio image-editing software, which can be used to produce color proofs of images that will ultimately appear in the DesignStudio page layout.

Ventura Publisher

The Macintosh version of Ventura Publisher, released late in 1990, was one of the most eagerly anticipated software products to reach the Apple platform. Ventura, originally introduced for the DOS environment, quickly became a bestseller among PC users thanks to its automated approach to production of books and other long documents. Though the Macintosh market includes numerous capable desktop publishing packages, few offer the long-document capabilities available in Ventura. The new version also offers the possibility of using Ventura in an environment served by a plethora of sophisticated graphics applications.

Ventura Publisher for the Macintosh is nearly identical to its siblings in the IBM environment.

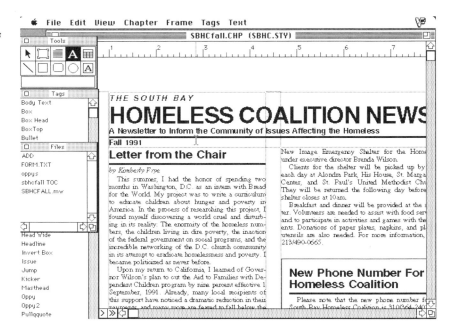

In keeping with the developer's cross-platform strategy, Ventura for the Macintosh is nearly identical to its siblings in the IBM environment. You can exchange most chapter files and style sheets with PC users running the DOS or Windows versions of the package. The similarity also makes Ventura Mac easy to learn for users who are already comfortable with the other versions.

For all the similarities with its siblings, Ventura Mac is unique in a few respects. It offers the basic look and feel that Macintosh users are familiar with, and includes an "Undo" function that is not available in the other versions. It also offers improved support for Macintosh text and graphics formats, though it cannot import (or separate) a color TIFF file. One nice feature is the ability to "Apply" changes made to a tag definition without leaving the dialog box. This lets the user "try out" a certain typographic effect to see how it looks. You can also navigate all the Style menu options (typographic effects, breaks, spacing, special effects, etc.) before implementing the style change. This makes the process of designing style sheets much more efficient.

Ventura Mac is clearly aimed at production of books and other long documents. Its color publishing functions are weak, and it lacks the kind of interactive design muscle found in programs like QuarkXPress or DesignStudio. However, it compares quite well with FrameMaker and Interleaf Publisher in its long document functions, and it benefits from a large cottage industry in add-on products, services, and training programs. The product is most appropriate for existing Ventura users who have Macs or want to exchange files with Macintosh users. It should also be considered as an alternative to FrameMaker or Interleaf Publisher by Macintosh users who need a tool for producing long documents.

Interleaf Publisher

Interleaf Publisher has its origins in a complex technical publishing system that runs on Unix-based workstations. Several years ago, Interleaf adapted the software to run on Macintosh II computers, and later to run on PC compatibles as well. And therein lies the strength and weakness of the package. Unix packages tend to be all-in-one applications, and Interleaf's software was no exception, with built-in text-editing, page layout, graphics, and document management functions. But in the microcomputer world, publishing is a cooperative affair that integrates files created with various software packages. Because of its origins in the Unix environment, Interleaf Publisher is not geared toward working with other software packages. And though it makes a stab at conforming to the graphical interface of the Macintosh, it also deviates from this in many important ways, such as its use of pop-up menus. The program is also designed for a two-button mouse, with many functions that require that the user click on the second button. Because the Macintosh mouse does not include a second button, users must hold down the command key as they click to simulate one.

Since its original Macintosh release, Interleaf's developers have improved the program in one key area: price. First introduced at a price of $2495, the package now lists for $995, bringing it closer to competing desktop publishing products like PageMaker and QuarkXPress. The original package required six megabytes of memory, but the current version gets by with two. This is somewhat deceptive, however. The program runs within two megabytes of RAM only by using a virtual memory function. Virtual memory is a scheme where the hard disk is treated as a section of memory. Sections of the program that would otherwise be held in RAM are instead swapped to and from the disk. Because disk access is much slower than RAM, performance suffers considerably on machines that have less than five megabytes of memory.

Still, Interleaf Publisher offers many powerful features for creating documents, especially long technical documents. Its text editing functions rival those in dedicated word processors, and it also provides a wide range of tools for creating graphic objects. A photographic image editor allows a variety of image manipulation operations, such as contrast adjustment, pixel editing, and rotation. However, the program cannot produce spot or process color.

One of the package's major strengths is its document management functions, which include outlining, indexing, and table-of-contents generation. Documents can be linked so that changes made to one will be made to others within the local area network. You can also track revisions made to documents on the network.

Interleaf has done much to improve this package since its original release, addressing many of the complaints that arose from users and reviewers. However, the program has failed to attract a following among Macintosh users, who still prefer QuarkXPress and PageMaker.

FrameMaker

Frame Technology's FrameMaker, like Interleaf Publisher, is derived from a technical publishing package first offered for Unix-based workstations. But Frame has managed to make a relatively smooth transition to the Macintosh. There are two principal reasons for this. First, FrameMaker, even in its workstation implementation, had a "look and feel" that was much closer to the Mac than Interleaf's interface. It was thus easier for the developers to conform with the Macintosh approach to software design. Second, the developers did more than just adapt the software to the new computer. Instead, they built it from the ground up to run on the Macintosh.

The result is a powerful, wide-ranging publishing package that manages to fit comfortably within the Macintosh environment. Unlike Interleaf Publisher, it works with a single-button mouse, and its general menu structure is similar to other Macintosh applications.

Like Interleaf Publisher and Ventura Publisher, FrameMaker's forte is long documents, such as books. Its style sheet function allows for automatic application of character and paragraph formatting to selected blocks of text. Styles can also be imported from a word processor. Multiple chapters—even those hundreds of pages long—can be linked into a single book. The program also supports list and table-of-contents generation, and can produce a six-level index. You can also enter cross-references, which are automatically updated as pagination changes. Another nice feature is the ability to mix landscape (wide) and portrait (tall) pages within the same publication. A powerful built-in formula editor makes the program useful for technical documents. The program's table-building functions are also powerful.

Though text can be imported from a word processor, FrameMaker includes a powerful built-in text editor that can be used for all but the most extensive text entry. It also features a built-in spell checker and a powerful search-and-replace function. For example, you can search for one style tag and replace it with another in addition to replacing body text. Hyphenation functions are also strong. The program uses a hyphenation algorithm along with a 130,000-word dictionary and a user dictionary. Users can also determine the maximum number of consecutive hyphens.

The program includes a basic set of tools for creating object oriented graphics, including Bezier curves. You can also import images in MacPaint, TIFF, PICT, and EPS formats. You can import color images, and apply one of eight colors to an object.

In short, FrameMaker does not offer every function a publishing user may desire. However, it is a powerful tool for producing long documents that is nevertheless easy to learn and use considering its complexity. Included with the package are templates and style sheets for producing books, newsletters, and other common documents.

Publish It

Publish It, from Timeworks Inc., is yet another entry in the market for Macintosh desktop publishing packages. The developer, which also offers a low-end, GEM-based publishing package by the same rather unfortunate name, has substantially upgraded the software for the Macintosh environment. In addition to its page layout features, Publish It offers a number of unique graphics and editorial functions. But it also has a few limitations that place it a notch below competing packages like PageMaker and QuarkXPress.

The most noticeable difference between Publish It and its Macintosh competition is its wide array of graphics tools. The toolbox, in addition to page layout functions, includes tools for creating bit-mapped and object-oriented graphics. This gives the interface a rather cluttered look, but many users will no doubt appreciate the ability to edit images from within the program.

The program's basic approach to page layout is similar to that used in Ready,Set,Go. Text and graphics files are placed into boxes drawn on the page. A linking tool is used to jump text from one block to another. Unlike the competition, however, the program cannot automatically flow text from one page to another, making it rather tedious to create large documents (the developer does provide a workaround for this, but it is still rather cumbersome).

Text can be imported in ASCII, MacWrite, WriteNow, Microsoft Word, and WordPerfect formats. Most basic formatting characteristics, such as font, type style, and line and paragraph spacing, are retained when text is imported.

Publish It's typographic features include automatic kerning, vertical alignment, and several leading options. Text can be stretched, rotated (in one-degree increments), and flipped. You can also wrap text around irregular objects, or even have it flow within a graphic object placed on the page. Some of the text-formatting options, however, seem like little more than gimmicks. For example, you can set the horizontal alignment so that the text fills odd shapes, such as a pyramid or "V" shape. This feature seems a lot less useful than widow or orphan control, which is missing from the package.

Editorial features in the program include search-and-replace, a 160,000-word spell-checker, and a 240,000-word thesaurus. In addition to searching for misspelled words, the spell-checker can be set up to flag mistakes as they are entered. We would not recommend this package as a standalone word processor, but these functions are helpful for correcting mistakes or making last-minutes changes after a document has been imported and edited.

Publish It includes a limited style sheet feature that allows you to create paragraph tags with specifications for font, type size, spacing, alignment, and other attributes. This is done by selecting a paragraph with the desired attributes, then entering a tag name. You can then apply that tag to other paragraphs to have them conform to the same style. If you tag a paragraph with a particular style, all subsequent paragraphs will use that style unless you specify otherwise.

Paint tools include a spray can, pencil, eraser, paintbrush, and flood fill. Though the default resolution for bit-mapped images created with the program is 72-dpi, you can specify any other resolution up to 300-dpi. A graphic conversion tool converts imported images (or text) into 72-dpi bit maps that can be edited with the paint tools.

Publish It's developers have also shown that certain graphics features are well at home in a publishing package. For example, all elements on the page, including text frames, are treated as objects that can be grouped or aligned. This is a very helpful feature that allows you to associate rules and other graphic elements with text frames that can then be moved as a single unit. You can specify the size and position of elements with great precision by entering measurements in a dialog box. You also have a lot more flexibility in creating rules and borders than permitted by competing packages, such as PageMaker. For example, you can add arrows to the ends of rules, a useful feature for creating diagrams.

PC-Compatible Programs

Aldus PageMaker

Aldus PageMaker has long held the distinction of being one of the few publishing packages available for both Macintosh and IBM-compatible computers. The IBM PC version of PageMaker, which runs under Microsoft Windows, is nearly identical to the Macintosh version.

Before the introduction of Windows 3.0 in 1990, PageMaker was hampered by limitations in the graphical environment that caused generally poor performance. However, Windows 3.0 introduced a new memory management scheme that improved this situation considerably. Given Windows' popularity, many developers have introduced new hardware and software products that directly or indirectly enhance the use of PageMaker. Several companies, including Adobe and Bitstream, have introduced products that vastly improve the on-screen appearance of type within any Windows application while reducing disk storage requirements for fonts. Others have introduced new graphics packages that can produce files for use with PageMaker.

Beyond the enhancements to the operating environment, PageMaker for the PC is virtually identical to the Macintosh version of the program. It includes the same pasteboard interface, which generally makes the program easier to learn and use than its chief competition, Ventura Publisher. Text and graphics are imported by means of the "Place" command, and an on-screen toolbox includes functions for entering text, cropping graphics, and adding rules, ellipses, and boxes. The style

The IBM PC version of PageMaker, which runs under Microsoft Windows, is nearly identical to the Macintosh version.

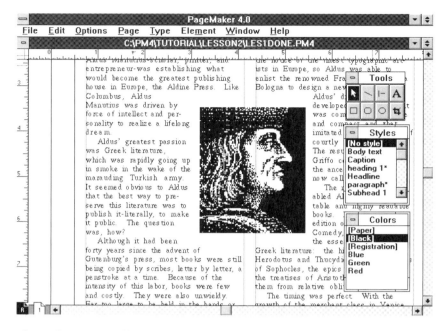

sheet function allows creation of style tags that include settings for typeface, type size, type style, paragraph spacing, and other variables. To apply the style to a paragraph, you place the cursor anywhere within and click on the tag name in a style palette that appears on the screen.

Ventura Publisher

Since its original release, Ventura Publisher has occupied a leading position among desktop publishing packages for IBM-compatible computers. Though it is not the easiest program to learn, it can be quite productive once you master its approach to document design. It is especially strong for producing books, reports, and other long documents with a consistent format. However, it can also be used for producing newsletters, flyers, and other design-intensive publications.

The program was originally developed by a small California company called Ventura Software, which sold the marketing rights to Xerox Corp. Xerox then sold the package as "Xerox Ventura Publisher." Since then, a new Xerox subsidiary—also called Ventura Software—has taken over development of the product, which is now known simply as "Ventura Publisher."

Ventura is a powerful piece of publishing software. The core of the program is a robust style sheet function that automates document production. Each style sheet consists of tags that include a wide range of formatting information. For example, you can define a "bullet" tag that automatically adds a bullet to a paragraph along with any other formatting you desire. The formatting options also offer a high degree of control over character spacing, rules, and indents. Tags can be applied to paragraphs from within the program, or entered as bracket codes within a word processor. In the latter case, the text file is automatically formatted once it is imported into Ventura.

In addition to the style sheets, Ventura uses a frame-based approach to page layout. A frame is a block on the page layout that can contain text or graphics. Each page has an "underlying" frame for text placement, but you can also add smaller frames. The program makes it easy to place text and graphics within a frame.

Beyond the style sheets and frames, Ventura offers a wide range of powerful functions that automate long document production. These include cross-references, indexes, table-of-contents generation, vertical justification, and automatic numbering of pages, chapters, and sections. With the Professional Extension, you can create complex tables or mathematical and scientific formulas from within the program.

Another strength in the program is its ability to run on inexpensive computer systems—a tribute to the GEM graphical environment under which it operates. Relatively simple documents can be created on an XT-clone with just 640K of memory. However, a more powerful computer with extended memory is recommended for complex projects with a lot of graphics or those that require maximum productivity. If you do run it on a 286 or 386 machine, you will find performance to be excellent. Ventura also does a good job of economizing on disk storage. Instead of storing all document information within the chapter file, the program adds "pointers" that link the chapter to constituent text and graphics files created with other packages. Any changes made to the text from within Ventura are automatically reflected in the original word processing file.

Ventura Publisher Windows Edition

The Windows version of Ventura Publisher was developed in response to the enormous popularity of Windows 3.0. When it was first released in 1990, it had much in common with the DOS version with a few exceptions, including a redesigned menu structure and on-line help. The program's toolbox, tag list, and file list, which were fixed in a sidebar in the DOS version, were displayed as windows that could be moved and resized. And instead of requiring that users enter a Graphics mode to draw lines, boxes, or circles, the program presented these tools as part of the standard toolbox. However, the program also suffered from slow performance and numerous bugs that sometimes caused it to quit unexpectedly. Many users who eagerly awaited the Windows edition were disappointed with this initial release, and most stuck with the GEM version.

Ventura has since introduced a new Windows version of Ventura that addresses many of the limitations in the original release. The company has also added some powerful color extensions that allow the user to scan color images directly into a document, touch them up with a color image editor, and then produce color separations on a high-resolution imagesetter.

Interleaf Publisher

IBM Interleaf Publisher has much in common with its Macintosh sibling, including the ability to run within two megabytes of memory. Like its companion product, it takes an all-in-one approach to publication production, offering extensive tools for text editing, graphics, page layout, and document management.

Interleaf Publisher offers many powerful features, especially for creation of long technical documents. Its text editing functions rival those in dedicated word processors, and it also provides a wide range of tools for creating graphic objects. Document management functions are also strong, with support for outlining, indexing, and table-of-contents generation. The program also offers extensive support for local-area networks, including LANs from 3Com and Novell. Among its typographic features are a powerful hyphenation function, widow and orphan control, and vertical justification.

The graphics mode offers 16 levels of magnification, but otherwise you are limited to viewing the page at the actual size. Other views, such as fit-in-window or facing pages, are not supported.

With the introduction of Microsoft Windows, IBM-compatible computers have suddenly become hot items for development of publishing and graphics applications. Existing programs, such as Ventura Publisher and PageMaker, already meet or exceed Interleaf's capabilities in many areas.

Finesse

Logitech's Finesse is a relatively modest desktop publishing package for IBM-compatible computers. Users of Ventura Publisher or PageMaker won't find reason here to give up their favorite applications, but others will find it an inexpensive and easy-to-learn package for producing simple publications like newsletters, reports, or brochures. As such, it fits in nicely with Logitech's hardware products, which include a successful line of mice and an inexpensive hand-held scanner.

Like the DOS edition of Ventura Publisher, Finesse runs under GEM. One of GEM's advantages over Windows is that it performs well on older, slower XT and AT computers that would have the Microsoft environment crawling. Its modest hardware requirements and low cost provide an inexpensive ticket to desktop publishing for novice users.

Finesse also has some resemblance to PageMaker. This is most noticeable in its use of left and right master pages for repeating design elements, but it is also apparent in the program's general interactive approach. To design a page, you create individual frames in which text and graphics are placed. Text, however, cannot be automatically "poured" from page to page as it can with Ventura. Finesse also lacks style sheets, though you can copy type and spacing attributes from one paragraph to another.

Finesse includes a simple text editor, but it is much more productive when working with text files produced by a separate word processor. When you create a text frame, a dialog box prompts you for a file name in one of six formats: ASCII, WordStar, First Word Plus, GEM Write, WordPerfect, or Microsoft Word. Text is flowed from frame to frame by means of a chain tool that links them together. When you select a section of text for formatting, a box appears allowing you to choose a type style: normal, bold, italics, and so on. Other text and paragraph formatting options are found in a Text menu. Though Finesse doesn't present all the formatting options found in high-end packages like Ventura, the basic functions are included.

A Tab Position box lets you set up to eight tab stops. You are limited to left-aligned or decimal tabs, and you cannot choose leader characters, such as lines or periods. This last omission would be a problem if you wanted to create a coupon with fill-in blanks or a table of contents with leader periods. Finesse also includes a simple kerning feature for loosening or tightening a string of characters, but it works only in one-point increments. High-end packages generally let you work in fractions of a point.

Printing functions are handled by the GEM output module, a separate program accessed when you select the Print command. The module supports print spooling and offers a wide range of output drivers, including PostScript.

Finesse is one of several "entry-level" publishing packages that are relatively simple and inexpensive. Others in this category include Express Publisher from PowerUp Software, Avagio from Unison World, and Microsoft Publisher, a relatively new Windows-based application from Microsoft.

Legacy

NBI's Legacy is one of a new breed of software packages that combine desktop publishing and word processing functions. It has its origins in an earlier program called Legend, a Windows application that proved to be slow and cumbersome. Legacy, on the other hand, takes advantage of new memory management functions in Windows 3.0 that improve performance considerably. The result is a package that deserves consideration by anyone who needs an all-in-one tool for creating attractive documents.

Legacy has a comprehensive set of features. These include spell-checking, search-and-replace, cross-referencing, index and table-of-contents generation, mail merge, style sheets, auto-numbering, and a table editor. It also includes tools for creating simple graphic objects, such as boxes, lines, and circles. The downside is that Legacy is a complex and not entirely intuitive program. With some publishing packages, an intelligent user can figure out many of the features simply by navigating around the screen.

Combining word processing and page layout features is not as easy as it may sound. Word processing packages are geared toward rapid, productive entry and editing of text, while desktop publishing packages are geared toward integration of text and graphics into a page layout. Though you can enter text in a desktop publishing package, this is often unproductive because the program has to redraw the screen—complete with graphics and text formatting—whenever changes are made. Legacy gets around this by offering multiple display modes. In "draft view," all you see is unformatted text, along with codes that indicate the formatting that would appear in the layout. "Detail view" shows the page layout, with formatted text and graphics, plus non-printing elements such as paragraph markers. "Proof view" shows the document exactly as it will be printed. This is similar to the approach used by Samna's Ami and Microsoft's Word for Windows, two other packages that combine word processing and desktop publishing features.

Like Ventura Publisher, Legacy uses frames and style sheets as the basic elements of page layout. There are four categories of frames: text, table, graphic, and EPS (used to display an imported Encapsulated PostScript file). Supported text formats include ASCII, Microsoft Word, Multimate, Word Perfect, and WordStar. Supported graphics formats (in addition to EPS) include PCX, MSP, MacPaint, TIFF, CGM, and Windows Metafile. Table data can be imported in DIF, WKS, and WK1 formats.

Each page automatically includes a "page frame," but you can also add smaller "dependent frames" to the page. Each frame is defined by a "property set," similar to a style tag, that determines its margins, borders, and other attributes. These property sets can be saved and applied to other frames. Another nice feature is the ability to change the page frame orientation from portrait to landscape (or vice versa) for a single page within the document.

The style sheet feature is also powerful, allowing the user to define styles that include text formats, ruling lines or boxes, spacing attributes, bullets, and other settings. You can also define colors as part of the style, but this is not as useful as it may seem. Legacy can produce color output on a color printer, but it does not support color separations, even simple spot color overlays.

In addition to styles, Legacy uses "tokens" to format text. A token is a code that instructs the program to format text a certain way. Style tokens apply a particular style, but tokens can also define index entries, kerning commands, and text formats, such as boldface or italics. Using the "View Token" command, you can see the tokens embedded in the text, but you can also turn off the token display. You can also use tokens with the search-and-replace function, providing an easy way to change styles and other formatting instructions.

One of the program's major strengths is its document management functions. Outlines, footnotes, and pages can be automatically numbered. Tables-of-contents and three-level indexes can be automatically generated. You can also produce up to 15 automatically generated lists in addition to the index and table of contents.

Chapter Five

Illustration and Drawing Programs

Graphics programs used in desktop publishing systems fall into two general categories. Painting and image-editing programs create graphics in the form of tiny dots. These graphics are known as "bit-mapped" or "raster" images. Illustration and drawing programs create graphics in what is known as an "object-oriented" or "vector" format. These images consist of objects—curves, lines, and shapes—that can be combined into complex illustrations.

On the computer screen, object-oriented images appear to be no different from standard bit-mapped images. But the software sees the objects much differently: as mathematical expressions instead of an array of dots. One way to understand the difference is to consider a simple picture, such as a stop sign. In a bit-mapped format, the stop sign would be a series of dots organized into an octagon. In an object-oriented format, the stop sign would be stored as a series of mathematical instructions: go right for six inches, then at a 45 degree angle for 6 inches, then another 45 degree angle for 6 inches, and so on.

Object-oriented images offer a number of advantages over bit-mapped images. Because they are described in mathematical terms, the software can print them at the maximum resolution of the output device. You can print the stop sign at 300 dots per inch on a laser printer or produce the same image at 3000 dots per inch or more on a PostScript imagesetter. If the stop sign is produced as a 300-dpi bitmap, it will print at that same resolution even on a 3000-dpi imagesetter. Object-oriented images can also be enlarged or reduced without loss of image quality.

Another benefit of object-oriented images is implied by the phrase used to describe them. When you draw a square, the software sees it as a discrete object that can be moved, rotated,

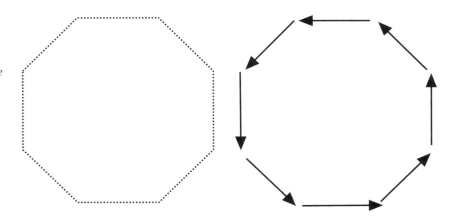

In a bit-mapped format, the stop sign is a series of dots. In an object-oriented format, the sign is a series of mathematical instructions: go right for six inches, then at a 45 degree angle for 6 inches, then another 45 degree angle for 6 inches, and so on.

stretched, or otherwise manipulated without affecting other objects in the image. Objects can be filled with various patterns or colors and grouped with other objects to create complex illustrations.

The first popular software package capable of producing object-oriented graphics was Apple's MacDraw (now sold by Apple software subsidiary Claris Corp.). But the first package to take full advantage of the power of object-oriented graphics was Adobe Illustrator, originally released in 1987. Its power came in part from its use of "Bezier curves," a curve or line defined by control points that determine its size, shape, and direction. By moving these control points, you can manipulate Bezier curves into any form desired. Illustrator also allowed users to import bit-mapped images for tracing purposes. A faded-out version of the bit-mapped image appeared on the screen, allowing the user to trace over it with object-oriented graphics tools as if drawing over tissue paper.

Once you created an object on the screen, it could be easily moved, rotated, stretched, or scaled. You could also produce a mirror image of the object, or group it with other objects. Objects could also be filled with various patterns or colors. However, Bezier curves also proved to be difficult to master. Instead of just drawing the object on the screen, you had to manually place each control point and manipulate them to produce the desired shape.

The current generation of illustration packages, including Illustrator, have gone far beyond these original capabilities. Instead of requiring manual placement of control points, all of the leading illustration packages include a "freehand" tool that allows automatic creation of Bezier curves. You simply draw a

Object-oriented images can be enlarged or reduced without loss of image quality. Here, the Panda's nose was enlarged as an object-oriented image (middle), and as a bit-mapped image (bottom).

curve on the screen, and the program adds the control points as appropriate. You can then adjust the points as necessary.

Type-handling capabilities in illustration packages have also been improved. You can enter a headline on the page layout, then change the shapes of the characters as if they were graphic objects. Some illustration programs have enhanced their typographic capabilities to the point where they can be used as simple desktop publishing packages, producing flyers, advertisements, and even simple newsletters.

Illustration packages have also improved their ability to work with bit maps. In addition to importing bit-mapped images for tracing purposes, you can incorporate them directly into the illustration. Autotracing functions allow automatic conversion of bit-mapped images into an object-oriented format.

Some programs offer extra features that make it easier to produce certain kinds of special effects. Blending functions, for example, allow creation of transitional effects between two objects. You select the objects, then instruct the program to blend one into the other, specifying the number of transformational objects to be placed between them. For example, you can select two squares, one black and one white, and have the program generate a series of squares shaded with lighter and lighter levels of gray. You can also blend different shapes into one another, converting a bird into a fish, for example.

Finally, most of the leading illustration packages can be used to produce color separations, either by themselves or in combination with a color separation utility.

Macintosh Programs

Illustration and drawing packages for the Macintosh include Adobe Illustrator, Aldus Freehand, Deneba's Canvas, MacDraw II, DeskDraw, and Aldus SuperPaint. Two of these, Canvas and SuperPaint, combine drawing and painting functions. Some packages aimed at working with type, such as Broderbund's TypeStyler and Letraset's FontStudio, offer graphics tools similar to what might be found in an illustration package. Letraset's ColorStudio includes a module called Shapes that offers object-oriented editing functions for type and other graphics.

The two leading Macintosh illustration packages are Illustrator and Freehand.

Adobe Illustrator

Adobe Illustrator remains a favorite among professional artists and designers. Its relatively simple menu structure provides access to powerful tools for creating a wide variety of images.

Like the original version of the program, Illustrator includes a pen tool for manually creating Bezier curves. But it also provides a freehand tool that allows you to draw a curve, then automatically places Bezier control points that define the curve's size and shape. Once objects are created, they can be resized, reversed, stretched, rotated, and otherwise manipulated as you desire.

Illustrator's text-handling capabilities are quite powerful. While most illustration programs require you to enter text in a dialog box before it is displayed on screen, Illustrator allows you to enter text directly into the illustration. You can also import text from a word processing package, allowing creation of flyers, advertisements, and even newsletters. With typographic fea-

Bezier curves are defined by control points that determine their size, shape, and direction. By moving these control points, you can manipulate Bezier curves into any form desired.

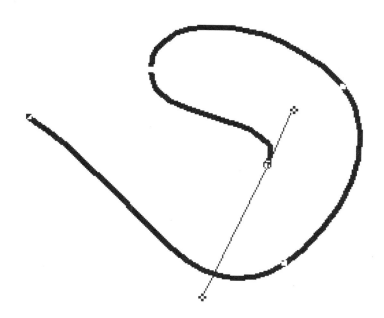

tures like tracking and space control, Illustrator can function as a simple desktop publishing tool. However, it also offers text-handling functions that no desktop publishing package can match. You can enter text so that it follows a curved or angled path, or have it fill an object in the layout. You can also convert text into outlines that can be manipulated as graphic objects.

Another unique feature is a graphing function that allows creation of column, line, pie, area, and scatter graphs. Data used to create a graph can be imported from a spreadsheet program or entered in a data window. Once the graph is created, it is treated as an object outline that can be manipulated with graphics tools. You can even create an object and define it as a graphing element. For example, you can create an illustration of a cow and use it as the "bar" in a bar graph on milk production.

Illustrator's autotrace tool can automatically convert bit-mapped images into an object-oriented format. The feature does not work perfectly, but it can provide a great head start if you need to produce an illustration quickly.

The program's color separation features are also strong. Using a utility program called Adobe Separator, which is supplied with Illustrator, you can determine whether the output will be positive or negative, whether the emulsion is up or down, and whether it is right-reading or wrong-reading. You can also use a transfer function to calibrate the output for a specific imagesetter. For example, if an imagesetter prints a 40-percent shade at 50 percent, you can adjust the output to correct this. You can also produce traps to compensate for misregistration, where colors shift slightly from one separation to the next when printed.

The major drawback in Illustrator is its implementation of the Preview mode. When you create or manipulate an object, you do so in a "wire frame" view where all you can see are the outlines of the object. To see the actual illustration with correct line widths, fill patterns, and colors, you must enter a Preview mode where you cannot edit the objects. This means you must keep two separate windows open—one for preview, one for editing—or switch back and forth between the two.

Aldus Freehand

Ever since the release of Freehand in 1988, Aldus and Adobe have engaged in a game of one-upmanship in which each seeks to match and exceed the features offered by the other. As a result, the two programs offer similar functions, though they are often implemented differently.

Freehand's major advantage over Illustrator is that you can create and edit illustrations in Preview mode. However, the program also offers a wire-frame display mode that offers faster performance. The other advantage of working in the wire-frame mode is that you can see underlying objects that would otherwise be obscured by objects in the foreground.

Freehand offers five basic tools for creating lines and curves: a freehand tool plus four different tools for placing Bezier control points. Transformation tools allow you to stretch, rotate, reverse, and resize objects. A style sheet feature allows you to create tags that define line widths, fill patterns, colors, and other graphic effects. You can then apply these tags to objects, making it easy to change their appearance.

One difference between Freehand and Illustrator is that Freehand allows up to 99 layers on which objects can be placed. This makes it easy to manage illustrations in which objects are drawn on top of one another. It also offers up to 100 levels of undo and redo, allowing you to retrace your steps in creating an illustration. Bit-mapped images in TIFF or MacPaint formats can be imported as tracing templates or to be printed as part of the image itself. You can also modify the brightness, contrast and gray-scale characteristics of imported images. A "Spread" option in the Print dialog box has the same effect as trapping.

Aldus Freehand, which was first available for the Macintosh, is also available in a Windows version.

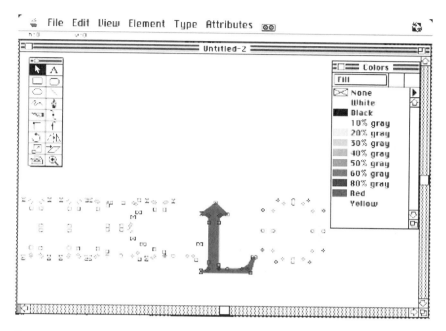

It enlarges the boundaries of basic fills and lines by a user-specified amount, reducing or eliminating any gaps that might appear due to poor registration on the printing press.

In addition to the Macintosh version of Freehand, Aldus has also introduced a Windows version that offers a nearly identical set of features.

IBM PC-Compatible Programs

The PC-compatible environment once lagged behind the Macintosh in offering professional-quality illustration packages, but this has changed in recent years largely due to the emergence of Microsoft Windows. The market for Windows-based illustration packages has become increasingly competitive, with packages from Corel (Corel Draw), Micrografx (Micrografx Designer), Computer Support Corp. (Arts and Letters), Aldus (Freehand), and Software Publishing Corp. (Harvard Draw). Digital Research offers an illustration package called Artline that runs under a graphical user interface derived from GEM. Adobe offers a Windows version of Illustrator, but despite the success of its Macintosh sibling, it has suffered from slow performance and is not considered a major factor in the market. The Windows version of Freehand, one of the most recent additions to the market, is pretty much identical to the Macintosh version.

Corel Draw

Corel Draw, from Corel Systems Corp., is generally considered to be the market leader among Windows-based illustration packages. This is due to its wide range of features, superior text-handling functions, and an easy-to-use interface. Almost all of the essential elements of a professional illustration tool are present: Bezier curves, a freehand drawing tool, bit-mapped image import, and the ability to produce four-color separations. Objects can be grouped, stretched, rotated, reversed, and manipulated in many other ways. Bit-mapped images in PCX or TIFF format can be imported as tracing templates or for inclusion in the layout as-is.

Corel Draw's text-handling features are among the most powerful of any illustration program. The package includes about 150 typefaces in Corel's own format. Most of these typefaces are equivalent to popular faces used in graphic design. When you produce a file, you can choose to have the type printed as a graphic or have the printer or imagesetter substitute the equivalent typeface. Each character can be reshaped as if it were a graphic object. You can also force a line of text to run along a curve or angle, or perform a variety of special envelope effects. If Corel Draw's typefaces aren't enough, the WFNBOSS utility included with the program allows conversion of Adobe and Bitstream typefaces into the Corel format.

An autotrace module called CorelTrace can be used to convert bit-mapped images into the Corel Draw format. The pro-

Corel Draw is a popular illustration program that runs under Windows.

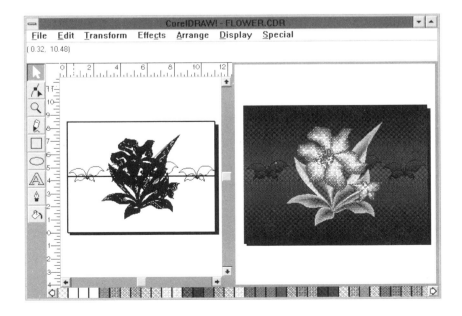

gram also supports a wide range of file formats for import and export. The Mosaic utility sold with the program allows users to view and catalog their image files. The package is also sold with a large collection of clip art.

Micrografx Designer

Micrografx Designer was one of the first illustration packages for DOS computers. Its publisher, Dallas-based Micrografx, has developed a number of successful graphics programs for Microsoft Windows, and is considered to have particular expertise in Windows development. It should not be surprising, then, that this Windows-based package has a lot to offer the professional artist, particularly those who produce technical illustrations.

With its precise measuring and positioning tools, Micrografx Designer has long been a favorite of technical illustrators. It can import and export CAD files, offers a library of graphic symbols, and can place objects on multiple layers. It can also be used to produce four-color separations.

Though Designer lagged behind Corel Draw in offering sophisticated type manipulation features, recent versions of the package can be used to create a variety of text effects. A Slide Show module allows users to set up on-screen presentations using artwork created with the program. A communications module allows users to transmit Designer files to slide-making service bureaus.

As with other illustration programs, objects created with Designer can be manipulated by a number of editing tools. One unique feature, however, is the ability to customize the toolbox. You can add or delete any function you wish, giving you quick access to the features you use most often. You can also create symbol libraries with commonly used images.

In addition to Designer, Micrografx also sells a low-cost illustration program called Windows Draw that includes many of the features in the more expensive package, including the ability to convert text into editable objects.

Arts and Letters

Arts and Letters, developed by Computer Services Corp. in Dallas, was once distinguished mostly by the large collection of clip art sold with the package. Its graphics tools, however, were notoriously weak in comparison with Designer and Corel Draw. However, later versions of the program brought it much closer to its competition, offering type manipulation, autotrace, color separation capabilities, and a high degree of flexibility in setting values for Bezier control points.

The program continues to offer a wide range of clip art, which can be imported into an illustration using a special dialog box. However, you have to use a printed directory to look up the code number for each piece of clip art before it can be imported.

Like Micrografx, Computer Support Corp. offers a low-cost, entry-level version of its illustration software. The program, known as Apprentice, includes a large clip art collection along with basic drawing tools.

GEM Artline

GEM Artline, from Digital Research Inc., is unique in that it does not run under Microsoft Windows. One advantage of this is that it can theoretically run on older XT- and AT-compatible computers that cannot run Windows. However, a 386 machine is recommended to take full advantage of the program.

Artline includes most of the basic features that have defined the professional illustration software category: Bezier curves, free rotation of objects, stretching, scaling, and other editing functions. Its symbol libraries can be customized to include any desired graphic images. Images are displayed in a sidebar and can be quickly pasted into an illustration. It was also one of the first illustration packages to emphasize type-handling features. Still, the program has had trouble establishing itself

Software Publishing Corp.'s Harvard Draw is a new entry in the Windows market.

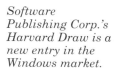
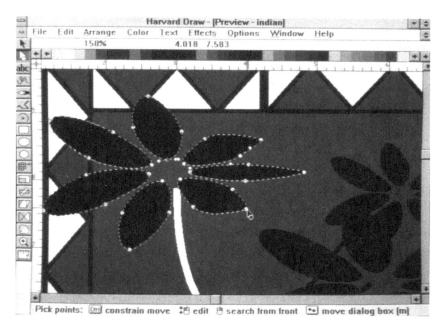

given the success of Corel Draw, Micrografx Designer, and Arts and Letters.

Harvard Draw

Harvard Draw, from Software Publishing Corp., is one of the most recent entries in the Windows illustration category. Its developers have included most of the features found in competing illustration packages: Bezier curves, freehand drawing, autotrace, and more. However, it also offers some features unique to the PC illustration market, such as the ability to create graphics in preview mode, multiple layers, and multiple levels of undo and redo. You can also enter text directly on screen and edit it as if it were a graphic object. The program is sold with 47 typefaces from Bitstream.

Now that we've seen how illustration software can improve the desktop publishing process, it's time to move on to the other type of image: photographs. The next three chapters will cover this topic in detail.

Chapter Six

Scanning Images

Desktop scanners represent one of the fastest-growing hardware categories in the desktop publishing market. These "electronic eyes" can convert images on paper and film into a digital format. They are used to "capture" photographs, line art, text, and other images that can then be manipulated with computer software.

Scanners come in a wide variety of formats, capabilities, and price ranges. The type of scanner you purchase depends on what kinds of images you want to capture. If your image-capture needs are limited to line art or text, you can get away with a relatively simple model. If you want to capture black-and-white photographs to produce halftones, you need a gray-scale scanner. If you need to capture color images, you need a color scanner.

Gray-Scale Images

Without gray-scale capability, a scanner sees images in stark contrast: each dot is either black or white. In a normal photograph, however, a nearly infinite range of grays can be seen, enough so that neighboring gray shades appear to blend smoothly into one another. For a scanner to do an adequate job of recognizing a photograph, it must be able to sense variable shades of gray. But it does not need to recognize an infinite number of gray shades. Most photographs need to show a range of 16 to 256 shades of gray between black and white to look realistic; the higher the number of gray levels, the better the reproduction generally will be.

Most gray-scale scanners sold these days can recognize up to 256 shades of gray. They are also known as "8-bit" scanners, since it takes eight bits of data to store up to 256 values. Older gray-scale scanners were limited to 4 bits (16 gray shades) or 6

The higher the number of gray levels in an image, the better the reproduction will be. The top image has two shades of gray: black and white. The image in the middle has 16 shades of gray and the bottom image has 256 shades of gray.

bits (64 gray shades). Some scanners without gray-scale capability are advertised as being able to produce halftones. However, these should be avoided. They use a form of dithering on the input end that severely limits the quality of the images they produce.

Color Images

All color scanners have one thing in common: they capture images as combinations of red, green, and blue. Depending on their capabilities, they can sense anywhere from 4 to 12 bits of information for each of these colors. Some scanners capture the red, green, and blue elements in three separate passes. Others can capture all three in a single pass.

Color scanners are distinguished by their resolution and a property known as "pixel depth," which is the color equivalent of gray-scale capability. But the way these specifications are used varies depending on the type of scanner. In hand-held and flatbed scanners, resolution is measured in dots per inch. But with slide scanners, resolution is measured in terms of the total number of vertical and horizontal lines.

Pixel depth refers to the number of shades of each color the scanner can recognize. Thus a 24-bit scanner recognizes 8 bits per pixel (256 shades) for each component color in the image—red, green, and blue (these component colors are sometimes referred to as "channels"). The result is an image that can contain up to 16.8 million different colors. Some of the more expensive slide scanners actually go beyond this, scanning at up to 12 bits (4096 total shades) per channel. They do this because random "noise" reduces the amount of usable color data in the resulting image. By scanning at a higher pixel depth, the scanner can produce a 24-bit color image that more accurately represents the original.

Types of Scanners

Beyond their image-capture capabilities, scanners used in desktop publishing systems fall into four categories: hand-held, flatbed, slide, and drum.

Hand-Held Scanners

In the low end of the scanner market, hand-held devices priced at $250 to $500 have carved a significant niche for themselves. These scanners are produced by Asian manufac-

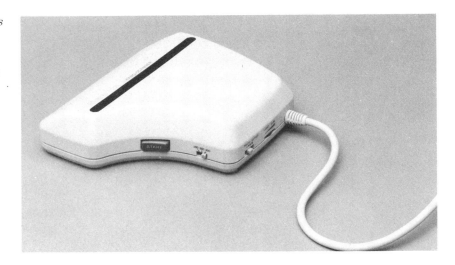

turers like Mitsumi, then sold under various brand names by U.S. companies. They have their limitations, but their low prices make them a good choice if your scanning needs are limited to small line-art images. Many offer 200-dpi resolution, but several models with 300- and 400-dpi resolution are also available.

The major weakness in hand-held scanners, aside from a general lack of gray-scale or color capability (and reliance on the sometimes unsteady human hand), is their limited scanning area. Some can scan images up to four inches in width, but others are limited to two-and-a-half inch swaths.

Some manufacturers of hand scanners are beginning to offer color or gray-scale capability, but there are still limitations. Resolution is often limited to less than 100 dpi. Pixel depth is also limited. Some hand-held color scanners, for example, can sense just 16 gradations for each of the three primary colors. This compares with 256 gradations for other types of scanners.

Flatbed Scanners

Flatbed scanners offer resolutions ranging from 300 to 800 dpi, with most providing 300 to 400 dpi. In most models, a sensing device passes over the image three times, one each for red, green, and blue. They can theoretically sense up to 256 shades of each color, but distortions in the scanning process can reduce this to between 64 and 128 shades. Images captured by flatbed scanners can look washed out compared with traditional prepress output. But considering the price-to-quality

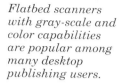

Flatbed scanners with gray-scale and color capabilities are popular among many desktop publishing users.

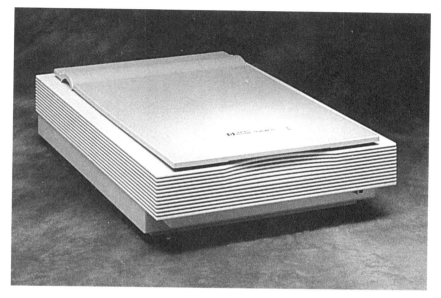

ratio, some publishers find that flatbed scanners are sufficient for their needs.

Flatbed scanners resemble small photocopiers, with a removable cover and glass platen. The user places a photograph on the platen, and an array of photosensitive sensors known as CCDs moves across the scanning area. Sheetfed or edge-fed scanners use rollers to pull the photograph over the CCD array, but these are not recommended for gray-scale image capture. Some hand-held scanners have gray-scale capability, but again are generally not suitable for quality image work. Slide scanners, which capture images on 35-mm slides, can be used to capture gray-scale images, but these are quite expensive and are intended largely for color work.

Slide Scanners

Slide scanners are the best choice for professional users who produce color separations of photographs. True to their name, they capture images stored on slides and transparencies, and produce images superior to what a flatbed scanner can produce from a color print. Resolutions range from about 1000 lines per slide to 5000 or more. Most slide scanners can sense 8 to 12 bits of information per color per pixel. Distortions in the scanning process reduce this somewhat, but slide scanners can still sense millions of different colors.

Slide scanners, when combined with color separation software and a suitable output device, come the closest to offering

Slide scanners are the best choice for professional users who produce color separations of photographs.

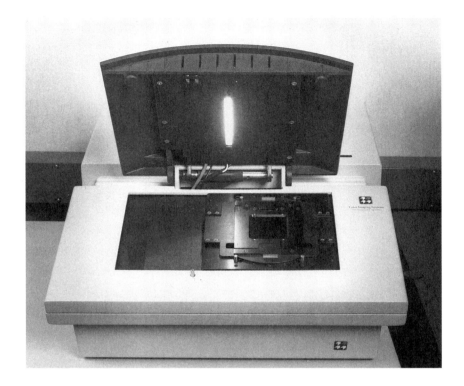

professional-level color publishing. The people at *National Geographic* and other publications that require high-quality color reproduction will probably want to stick with their current prepress systems. But for other users whose requirements are not quite as steep, these color scanners offer the possibility of bringing at least some of their production work in-house.

Other Scanners

With eight-bit flatbed scanners growing in popularity, sheetfed scanners seem to be on the decline. Though they are still suitable for many scanning tasks, sheetfed scanners cannot handle bound material and odd paper sizes. Flatbed scanners are also preferred when precise page alignment is needed. With price differentials between the two categories growing smaller and smaller, sheetfed devices will probably find themselves relegated to a few specialized tasks, such as scanning pages for transmission via PC facsimile.

Some companies offer scanners with unusual input mechanisms. Chinon, for example, sells an inexpensive device that uses an overhead scanning mechanism resembling an overhead projector. This allows you to place pages, books, or three-dimensional objects in the device's scanning bed. Truvel sells a scanner for professional graphics applications that uses a similar principle, though its resolution and gray-scale capabilities far exceed those of the Chinon device. At the low end, several companies sell scanners that attach to the print heads of dot-matrix printers. These products are extremely slow, however, and are not recommended for serious applications.

One product that occupies an area between flatbed and slide scanners is Truvel's TZ-3. This scanner, which includes color as an option, uses a camera-like mechanism that sits over a flatbed to capture images. Because of its design, it can capture three-dimensional objects in addition to images on paper. By using a zoom feature, users can increase the effective resolution to 900 dpi.

At the top of the price scale are digital drum scanners. These products use the same technology as the drum scanners found in traditional prepress systems. But instead of passing the image directly to the recording drum, the digital drum scanner stores the data in a digital format that can be imported into a computer system. Drum scanners offer the highest level of quality, but they are also quite expensive.

Video Digitizers

Digitizers are generally used to capture real-life three-dimensional images. They typically have two components, a video camera and frame-grabber board installed in the computer (though the frame-grabber alone is often referred to as a digitizer). The video camera records the image, while the frame-grabber converts it into a digital format. Once the image is converted, it is identical to an image captured by a scanner. Video digitizers should not be confused with digitizing tablets, which allow users to draw images using an electronic stylus and tablet.

A digitizer offers the ability to produce instant halftone images, since you don't have to bother with photo processing. But low-cost digitizers are generally limited in the quality of the images they can produce. They are also unsuitable for capturing images on paper. Digitizers that offer high-resolution image capture are quite expensive. Some scanners use a camera-like mechanism to capture images, and thus appear to be scanner/digitizer hybrids. Again, these tend to be more expensive.

Although video digitizers and frame grabbers represent the most common method of bringing traditional video images into a computer, they are not the only means. A company called

Video digitizers typically have two components, a video camera and frame-grabber board installed in the computer.

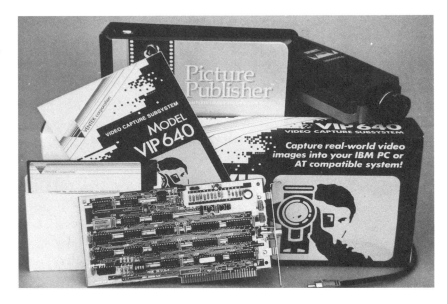

Dycam Inc. has recently released a still video camera that does away with the need for a video digitizer. Unlike traditional digitizers, which convert analog video frames into computer graphics files, the Dycam Model 1 camera creates and stores images in digital format. As a result, it need only communicate the digital link via a serial port to the IBM PC or Apple Macintosh.

The Dycam camera weighs less than 10 ounces and measures 3 inches by 6 inches by 1 inch deep. It comes with a battery recharger that holds a charge for about one day, or about 75 to 100 pictures. It stores up to 32 images in its electronic memory. Each picture is 376 pixels by 240 pixels with 256 levels of gray (8 bits). An electronic flash is built into the unit; exposure, flash, and focus are automatically determined.

Other than a simulated shutter—called a "trigger" on the Model 1—all the controls for the camera are handled in software on the Macintosh or IBM PC. To "develop" images stored in the camera, the user connects it to the AC adapter, which is attached to the serial port on the host computer. The software allows you to preview a "snapshot" of all 32 images stored in the camera. Any or all of the images can then be saved to disk in TIFF format. Once saved, the images can be edited with any image-editing program. Dycam ships a version of Astral Development's Picture Publisher with both the IBM and Macintosh versions. One interesting feature of Dycam's software is a timer function: You can set the camera to snap a

The Dycam Model 1 camera creates and stores images in digital format.

picture after a specified delay (the camera must be docked to the adapter for this to work).

Image-Capture Software

Some scanners include external controls for brightness and contrast, but for the most part, all scanning functions are controlled by software. When operating a scanner, users must concern themselves with settings for brightness, contrast, scanning area, scale factors, and resolution.

Brightness and contrast functions work much like the same controls on a TV set. Brightness adjusts the lightness or darkness of an image, while contrast adjusts the amount of difference between light and dark areas. The default settings for your scanner control software will usually work best, but sometimes you may want to make adjustments. An image that appears too dark may benefit from raising the brightness level. You may be able to bring out greater detail in washed-out photos by increasing contrast.

The scanning area is the actual portion of the photograph you want to capture. As we shall see, gray-scale images consume a lot of disk space. One way to reduce this is to capture only that part of an image you really need. Typically, this is done by drawing a box over a representation of the scanning area displayed on the screen. To assist in this effort, most scanner control programs allow you to perform a low-resolution "test scan" to preview an image before using it. You can select the appropriate portion in the preview and scan it at full resolution.

Scaling factors allow you to enlarge or reduce a photograph as it is being scanned. Though you can also do this afterwards in your desktop publishing or image-editing software, you generally get better image quality if you handle scaling on the initial scan. In most cases, scaling is measured in terms of percentages. If you scan an image at 100 percent, it is reproduced at its original size. An image scanned at 200 percent doubles in dimensions. An image scanned at 50 percent is cut in half. Most scanner control programs allow you to reduce images as much as you want. But if you want to increase image size, you generally have to reduce the resolution at which the image is scanned.

Image-Editing Packages

One factor driving the growth of the scanner market is the emergence of software packages meant to work specifically with scanned images. Though we have long had paint programs like MacPaint and PC Paintbrush that could edit black-and-white images, packages capable of editing photographic images are a more recent phenomenon.

The first of these image-editing programs, as they are called, were Letraset's ImageStudio and Silicon Beach Software's Digital Darkroom. These packages gave Macintosh users a wide range of tools for manipulating gray-scale images—images in which the dots could be variable shades of gray. With gray-map editing tools, you can convert an image to a negative or adjust the distribution of gray shades to improve its ultimate appearance. With cut-and-paste tools, you can remove the image of an executive from one office scene and insert it into another. Or, following the example in Digital Darkroom's user manual, you can "unlean" the Leaning Tower of Pisa. With convolution filters, you can sharpen or soften an image, or blur it completely out of recognition.

Since the release of ImageStudio and Digital Darkroom, several developers have introduced software packages that can manipulate color images. The most popular of these are Adobe Photoshop and Fractal Design's ColorStudio.

Astral Development's Picture Publisher, one of the first image-editing programs for DOS computers, provides the basic image-editing features found in its Macintosh cousins. First released as a gray-scale image editor, it is now capable of

Image-editing programs like Digital Darkroom provide a wide range of tools for manipulating gray-scale images.

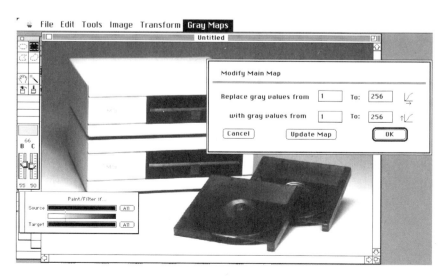

handling color images as well. Other image-editing packages for the PC environment include Aldus Photostyler, Image-In Color, and ZSoft's PhotoFinish.

Text Recognition

In addition to capturing images, scanners can also capture text. Using optical character recognition (OCR) software in conjunction with a scanner, you can convert pages from newspapers, magazines—or your typewriter—into text files that can be edited with a standard word processing program.

This segment of the software business has seen tremendous advances in a short time. As recently as 1987, most inexpensive OCR packages were limited to reading monospaced, typewritten text. Complicated jobs with typeset pages required dedicated hardware/software systems priced in the tens of thousands of dollars. But in the years that followed, low-cost OCR packages improved to the point where they now rival the most expensive text-recognition systems of the past.

The evolution of low-cost OCR began with simple packages like OCR Systems' ReadRight that could read only monospaced text. This limited their usefulness to automatic entry of manuscripts and other typewritten documents. The next step came with programs like Olduvai's Read-It that could recognize proportionally spaced, typeset text, but only after you "taught" the software to recognize that particular font. With this capability, you could scan pages out of a book, magazine, or newspa-

Optical character recognition (OCR) packages convert scanned documents into text files that can be edited with a word processor.

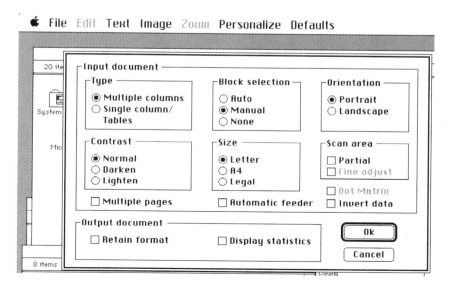

per. But given the time required for training, many users found it more efficient just to enter the text manually.

In offering these products, developers took advantage of the growing popularity of desktop scanners. Indeed, many OCR packages were bundled or offered as options with popular flatbed and sheetfed scanners. Many publishing users who purchased scanners for image acquisition found that they could also scan text simply by adding an inexpensive—if not terribly capable—software package.

At the same time, developers like Kurzweil (now Xerox Imaging Systems) and Palantir Corp. (now Calera Recognition Systems) had staked out the high end of the OCR market with dedicated text-recognition systems that combined software with scanning and processing software. These systems could recognize nearly any typeface with a high degree of accuracy, but they were also expensive, with prices commonly in the $50,000 range or above.

Then, in 1988, Caere turned the OCR market on its ear with OmniPage. This program, first introduced for the Macintosh and then for IBM compatibles, offered many of the sophisticated text-recognition capabilities found in the high-end systems. But at $895 for the original Macintosh version, OmniPage brought advanced OCR functions to the mass market of computer users. It continues to be the standard against which most other OCR products are measured.

The hallmark of OmniPage is its "omnifont" text recognition capability. Unlike the trainable packages, which must be taught to recognize individual typefaces, OmniPage could accurately read nearly any font without a time-consuming training process. It could also follow multiple-column layouts, and could even separate graphics from text.

There was only one fly in this ointment. Omnifont text recognition requires a lot of memory and processing power—which is why the high-end developers used dedicated hardware in the first place. OmniPage works with standard hardware, but requires four megabytes of memory on a Macintosh II or IBM-compatible 386 computer.

Since the introduction of OmniPage, other developers have scrambled to introduce their own inexpensive omnifont programs. Moving down from the high end, Xerox Imaging Systems now offers a version of the Kurzweil OCR software called AccuText, while Calera offers a similar package called WordScan. A special version of the Calera software is also offered by Hewlett-Packard as an option for the ScanJet Plus.

Though they have added lower-cost, PC-based products to their lineup, neither Xerox Imaging Systems nor Calera has abandoned the high end of the market. Both vendors target document-intensive installations such as scanning service bureaus, technical documentation departments, and insurance companies with their dedicated hardware/software systems.

In the meantime, OCR Systems (ReadRight), Inovatic (ReadStar), and other developers more commonly associated with the low end of the market have introduced their own OCR packages with omnifont capabilities. One newcomer, Recognita Corp. of Hungary, has received quite a bit of attention for its omnifont OCR software of the same name. Recognita also offers GO-CR, an OCR package designed for use with hand-held scanners.

Omnifont packages have pretty much killed the market for trainable OCR. In a trainable program, the software displays individual characters as a pattern of dots after the page has been scanned. The user then enters the correct character from the keyboard for that bit map. Eventually, the program builds an extensive type table for each font in its repertoire, usually with several bit maps for each character.

Even with the success of OmniPage, developers of trainable packages claimed that their products offered better accuracy on difficult-to-read typefaces while working within relatively modest hardware confines. But Recognita and ReadRight II both run on XT compatibles with as little as 640K of RAM. And several developers, including Caere, have added optional training functions to their omnifont packages. This means that you can "fine-tune" the software to recognize especially difficult characters or symbols. The new OmniPage Professional even lets you link symbols to terms of up to ten characters. For example, you can train the software to enter the word "box" when it recognizes a box (❑) in the text.

Now that most packages can recognize typeset text with little or no training, users must look to issues of accuracy, performance, hardware requirements, and other features when selecting OCR software.

Accuracy is obviously the most important variable. Most OCR packages claim accuracy of 99 percent or better, but even a 99 percent accuracy rate means one mistake every line or two on a standard typewritten page. A lower accuracy rate can make the package practically worthless. With the addition of training options in omnifont packages, users need to evaluate accuracy both on the first pass and after any fine-tuning. In some programs, the training option works only on that particular job; any trained characters are discarded for subsequent jobs. In other programs, the training is retained in a file similar to the user dictionaries found in spell-check software.

It is also important to realize that accuracy depends on the quality of the document (original vs. photocopy) and the particular typeface being recognized. Some typefaces—even those that appear normal at first glance—represent special challenges for OCR packages. Baskerville, for example, has a high crossbar on the lowercase "e" that causes some OCR programs to recognize it as a "c." Given that "e" is the most common letter in the alphabet, this can cause some serious problems with accuracy.

Performance is another important variable. After all, the whole point of purchasing an OCR package is that it allows you to enter text more productively. But measuring performance in an OCR package can be tricky given the various steps in the text recognition process. In most programs, the page is first scanned, then held in memory as the bit-mapped image is processed into a text file. By adding an automatic document feeder for multiple-page jobs, you can considerably speed up the first part. But the major bottleneck for most packages is text processing, which is dependent on memory and processor speed in addition to the capabilities of the OCR software.

OCR programs also vary in the range of scanners they support. Some can directly control dozens of scanners, which speeds up the text recognition process considerably. If your OCR program does not support your scanner, you need to first scan the page as a graphic, save it in a bit-mapped image format, and then use the OCR software to perform text recognition on the image file. This tends to reduce accuracy in addition to performance.

One recent trend is OCR software especially designed for hand scanners. Hand scanners, with their limited imaging areas and reliance on manual scanning, pose special challenges for OCR software. But they also make it easy to enter limited blocks of text from the page. Caere even offers a hand scanner/OCR combination called the Typist that works with virtually any PC-based software. The OCR software resides in memory; as text is scanned, it is placed into a text file as if entered from the keyboard.

Beyond these basic features, users should look for any functions that make a particular OCR package suitable for their needs. Some packages, for example, offer strong support for foreign languages.

Text editing capabilities represent another variable. Some packages allow you to edit text after it is scanned, while others require that you perform text editing in a separate word processor. Packages also vary in the range of file formats they support. Some are limited to saving text files in ASCII format plus a few popular word processor formats. Others support a wide range of word processors, plus spreadsheet formats. Still others allow you to generate style sheets for desktop publishing programs like Interleaf Publisher or Ventura Publisher. Spreadsheet support is helpful for converting tables into electronic worksheets, but the feature works best if the OCR software can scan in landscape mode.

Chapter Seven

Digital Halftones

The reproduction of photographs has been one of the most critical aspects of the graphic arts industry. With the advent of electronic publishing systems and desktop scanners, the nature of photographic imaging is changing dramatically. The difference is that halftone images are now being created in digital form. As we'll see in this chapter, this gives desktop publishing users and printers several new capabilities for enhancing and reproducing photographs.

In the traditional printing process, a halftone is created by shooting a photograph—also known as a continuous-tone image—through a fine film-based screen. What results is an image consisting of tiny dots. The dots can be square, round, or oval, but they are always spaced at even intervals. Dots in light areas of the image are very small, while dots in dark parts of the image are slightly larger. The varying dot sizes blend together and fool the unaided eye into perceiving continuous-gray shades. The halftone ends up looking much like the original photograph.

Desktop publishing systems have introduced a new kind of image known as the digital halftone. Typically, the process begins when the photograph is converted into a digital format by means of a desktop scanner. It ends on a piece of resin-coated paper or film produced by a PostScript imagesetter.

The quality of a halftone depends on several factors, the most important of which are resolution and gray scale. Resolution is determined by how closely the dots in the halftone screen are spaced. Desktop publishing users are accustomed to measuring resolution in dpi. But halftone resolution—also known as "screen frequency"—is measured in lines per inch, or lpi. Halftones with a high screen frequency have a high density of dots—and present a sharper image.

In most cases, halftones printed in newspapers are limited to

65 to 85 lpi because of the low quality of the newsprint on which they are reproduced. Magazine halftones generally offer 120 to 150 lpi, while fine art reproduction generally requires 200 lpi.

Gray scale, the other major factor affecting halftone quality, is a measure of the different levels of gray that an image can display. A continuous-tone image can show a nearly infinite range of gray values. Halftones simulate these continuous tones by varying the size of halftone dots. The number of possible dot sizes determines how many shades of gray can be shown in a particular image. In an image with 64 levels of gray, a dot can be any one of 64 sizes.

To look acceptable, a halftone needs somewhere between 64 and 256 levels of gray (plus one if you want to count white as a gray level). Images with an insufficient number of gray levels will appear to have distinct bands of gray rather than smoothly blended tones in transitional areas.

In addition to varying screen frequencies, halftones have different screen angles and dot shapes. The screen angle is defined as the orientation of halftone dots to the base of the screen. It is the angle measured from the base of the screen to an imaginary line connecting a row of dots in a direction that follows the shortest distance between the dots. For black-and-white and other single-color reproductions, the screen angle should be 45 degrees. The dot pattern is less apparent when the reproduction is at normal viewing distance, because people are accustomed to seeing in horizontal and vertical modes. Depending on the halftone screen used, dots can be round, square, or elliptical. Some halftone screens use lines instead of dots. Most halftones produced by desktop publishing systems have round dots.

Producing Digital Halftones

Halftones produced on a PostScript imagesetter are similar to those produced by traditional means. If you look at a digital halftone under a magnifying glass, it appears to consist of tiny dots of varying sizes, larger in dark areas and smaller in light areas. Like a traditional halftone, a digital halftone can have dots of varying shapes and angles. But the process for producing a digital halftone is much different than the traditional halftoning process.

Digital halftones can be produced on laser printers or high-resolution imagesetters. Like a printing press, these output devices are limited by their inability to produce dots with

*Halftones can use
various screen
angles, such as 0
degrees (top), 45
degrees (middle),
and 75 degrees
(bottom).*

varying intensity. But they have an additional limitation not shared with the printing press, for they cannot vary the size of the dots they print. A dot produced on a 300-dpi laser printer measures about one-three-hundredth of an inch. A dot produced on a PostScript imagesetter is also limited to the imagesetter's resolution, whether it's 1270 dpi or 2540 dpi. As we have seen, a traditional halftone gives the illusion of varying shades of gray by varying in size. To give the effect of variable-sized dots, digital output devices use a technique called "dithering."

Halftone Cells

So far, we have discussed halftone dots, which can vary in size, and digital dots, which cannot. Dithering introduces a third kind of dot that we'll call a halftone "cell." When a page layout program sends a dithered image to a laser printer, it groups two or more printer dots into a cluster—the halftone cell—that simulates one halftone dot. To avoid confusion in referring to these different kinds of dots, printer dots are sometimes known as "spots."

A halftone cell might consist of 64 spots arranged in an eight-by-eight square. The number of black printer dots determines the size of the halftone cell, and thus the amount of gray represented. If all printer dots are black, the halftone cell is black. If 48 out of 64 printer dots are black, the halftone cell appears dark (75 percent) gray. If 16 out of 64 printer dots are black, it's a lighter shade (25 percent) of gray.

With dithering we can get the appearance of gray scale, but

A dithered image consists of halftone cells, each of which contains an array of printer dots.

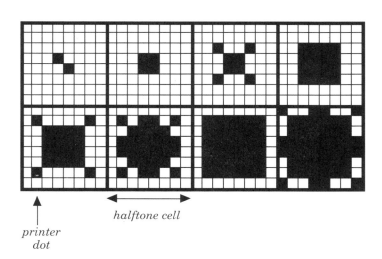

printer dot

halftone cell

at a cost in resolution. If you have a 300-dpi laser printer in which a four-by-four array is used in each halftone cell, resolution is cut—by a factor of four—to 75 lines per inch (lpi). This approaches the resolution you might find in newspaper photographs, but the 16 levels of gray provided by the clustering are below the minimum needed for realistic reproduction of an image. If you increase the number of gray levels to a more acceptable 64, effective resolution is reduced to about 50 lpi.

A laser printer with 300-dpi resolution produces barely acceptable halftones. But if you produce your pages on a high-resolution PostScript imagesetter, the resolution/gray scale trade-off becomes irrelevant. You could have halftone cells with 16 dots on a side, enough for 256 levels of gray, and still get a line screen of 150 lpi.

There is a relatively simple formula that can tell you the maximum screen frequency of a digital halftone given the number of gray shades and the resolution of the output device. Just take the square root of the number of gray shades and divide it into the resolution. If you have an image with 16 gray shades, the square root is four. Divide four into 300, and you get 75—the maximum screen frequency for most laser printers. An image with 256 gray shades produced at 2540-dpi resolution on an imagesetter can have a maximum resolution of slightly less than 160 lines. The square root of 256 is 16. Divide 16 into 2540 and you get 158.75.

To keep things simple, we've been dealing with nice round numbers—and assuming that the halftone dots will be printed in straight horizontal lines. But as we noted above, printers have found that halftones tend to look better when the dots are set off at 45-degree angles. This changes our numbers somewhat, but the trade-off between gray scale and resolution remains.

Capturing the Image

The process of producing a digital halftone begins with a desktop scanner or video digitizer. But not any scanner will do. As we learned in the previous chapter, the scanner needs gray-scale capability, meaning it can recognize multiple shades of gray in the images it captures. Most gray-scale scanners sold these days can recognize up to 256 shades of gray.

Most scanners and digitizers are sold with software that allows the user to control the image-capture process. Sometimes this is a stand-alone program that handles scanning and

When operating a scanner, users must concern themselves with settings for brightness, contrast, scanning area, scale factors, and resolution.

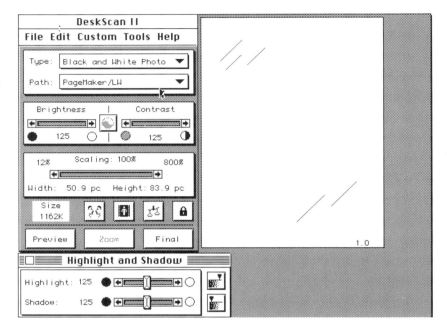

nothing else. Other programs include scanner control as part of a comprehensive set of image-editing functions.

Some scanners include external controls for brightness and contrast, but for the most part, all scanning functions are controlled by software. When operating a scanner, users must concern themselves with settings for brightness, contrast, scanning area, scale factors, and resolution.

Brightness and contrast functions work much like the same controls on a TV set. Brightness adjusts the lightness or darkness of an image, while contrast adjusts the amount of difference between light and dark areas. The default settings for your scanner control software will usually work best, but sometimes you may want to make adjustments. An image that appears too dark may benefit from raising the brightness level. You may be able to bring out greater detail in washed-out photos by increasing contrast.

The scanning area is the actual portion of the photograph you want to capture. As we shall see, gray-scale images consume a lot of disk space. One way to reduce this is to capture only that part of an image you really need. Typically, this is done by drawing a box over a representation of the scanning area displayed on the screen. To assist in this effort, most scanner control programs allow you to perform a low-resolution "test scan" to preview an image before using it. You can select the appropriate portion in the preview and scan it at full resolution.

Scaling factors allow you to enlarge or reduce a photograph as it is being scanned. Though you can also do this afterwards in your desktop publishing or image-editing software, you generally get better image quality if you handle scaling on the initial scan. In most cases, scaling is measured in terms of percentages. If you scan an image at 100 percent, it is reproduced at its original size. An image scanned at 200 percent doubles in dimensions. An image scanned at 50 percent is cut in half. Most scanner control programs allow you to reduce images as much as you want. But if you want to increase image size, you generally have to reduce the resolution at which the image is scanned.

Determining Optimal File Size

When producing scanned images for output on a PostScript imagesetter, you will be constantly faced with a trade-off between keeping the file to a reasonable size and achieving the best possible output quality. In general, the best strategy is to create a scanned image file that has as much image data as your output device can use. Since scanned images can take up a considerable amount of disk space and can slow the performance of an imagesetter, you don't want to create a scanned image with more data than can be appreciated by the human eye.

To determine the optimal file size for your image, you must know two things: the size of the final reproduced photograph, and the line screen of the reproduced photograph. The general formula for optimal file size is:

$$\text{File Size} = 2 \times (\text{Line Screen})^2 \times (\text{Size of Final Photo})$$

This formula assumes that you are using an 8-bit (256-gray level) scanner, which is highly recommended for producing images on a PostScript imagesetter. With an 8-bit scanner, each pixel consumes 1 byte (8 bits) of data. Thus, a 100-lpi halftone consumes $100 \times 100 = 10K$ bytes of data per square inch. (Note that there are $100 \times 100 = 10{,}000$ dots in a square inch; each dot consumes 1 byte). The factor 2 in the equation above results from the fact that you must provide more data than the bare minimum to compensate for various errors that come into the scanning process.

For example, imagine that you are going to scan a 4×5 inch photograph and reproduce it at the same size on a PostScript imagesetter using a 100-line screen. The optimal size, using the formula above, is then:

$$2 \times (100)^2 \times (4 \times 5) = 400 \text{ Kbytes}$$

What's important to note is that you can arrive at the 400K figure by varying either the scanning resolution or scale factor, or both. In the example above, we could have arrived at a 400K scanned image by scanning at 200 dpi and 100 percent scale factor, or we could have scanned at 100 dpi and 200 percent scale factor, or 300 dpi and 67 percent scale factor—each produces the same result.

Many scanner control programs, including DeskScan from Hewlett-Packard, show you the size of the file you are about to create, which makes it easy to adjust scale factor and resolution to arrive at the required file size.

Suppose instead that we had started with an 8×10 photograph, but still wanted the final image size to be 4×5 (50 percent reduction factor). How big should the file be? It should still be 400K—we have not changed the final image size or the line screen. You will find, however, that you can achieve the 400K file size by scanning at a lower resolution. In general, if you are reducing the size of a scanned image, you can lower the scanning resolution; if you are enlarging the image, you must increase the scanning resolution.

Also, notice that the amount of disk space required for an image increases geometrically as the size of the reproduced image increases. A halftone enlarged to 200 percent size requires four times as much data as the original. It's also a good idea to crop your image as you scan, rather than within the desktop publishing program. Although programs like Aldus PageMaker and QuarkXPress allow you to crop scanned images after you have placed them on a page, you will still be carrying around excess (though unseen) image data within your publication files.

If you use a digitizer, the issue of resolution is pretty much irrelevant. Since the number of pixels a digitizer can render is fixed, all images will appear at the same resolution. Factors like lighting and focus that are common concerns in photography are much more important.

Our discussion so far has focused on scanning continuous-tone photographic images. It is generally not recommended to scan an image that has already been converted into a halftone.

When the image is ultimately produced, the new halftone screen will conflict with the original screen, producing distortions known as moire patterns. If you absolutely must scan a halftone original, scan it as line art at full resolution in single-bit mode, and be careful not to scale it up or down.

Saving the Image

After an image is scanned, it is saved as a graphics file in one of several standard formats. Some scanner programs first scan an image into the computer's memory, after which it is saved as a file. This can cause problems if you don't have enough memory to handle the image data. Other programs can scan the image directly into a disk file.

The format you choose to store your image largely depends on the software you want to use it with. Obviously, you should not save an image in a format that's not supported by your image-editing or desktop publishing software.

TIFF, short for Tagged Image Format File, was developed by a small group of hardware and software developers as a standard file format for saving gray-scale images. It is supported by most leading publishing programs on the Macintosh and can be used with PC-based software as well. TIFF files can store images with up to eight bits per pixel, allowing a full 256 levels of gray. It is usually the preferred format for saving gray-scale images, since it is well supported by most software packages.

RIFF is a proprietary gray-scale file format developed for Letraset, which originally marketed DesignStudio, Ready,Set,Go, ImageStudio, and other programs. The major advantage of RIFF is that it allows compression of gray-scale images for reduced consumption of disk space. Its major disadvantage is that it works only with Letraset software. Users of Letraset packages may want to save their images in RIFF format, but others should choose TIFF.

PICT2 is an extension of Apple's PICT format for MacDraw and other draw-type programs. Unlike the original PICT format, PICT2 can save bit-mapped images with gray-scale information. However, even in the Macintosh environment, it is not as widely supported as TIFF.

Encapsulated PostScript, as we saw in Chapter Five, is a variant of the PostScript file format that can be used to store halftone images. However, it should be avoided unless you have no other alternative. EPSF files consume even more disk space than uncompressed TIFF files. And once saved in EPSF format, the image cannot be retouched or enhanced with image-editing software.

Editing the Image

After an image is saved, you may want to import it into an image-editing program. These programs, which include ImageStudio, Digital Darkroom, and Picture Publisher, are designed specifically for manipulation of gray-scale images produced on a scanner. Adobe Photoshop, a popular Macintosh application aimed at editing color images, can also be used to edit gray-scale images. In many ways, these programs are similar to paint packages like MacPaint or PC Paintbrush, but are geared toward images in which each dot can be one of several shades of gray.

The better image-editing programs can produce photographic effects previously achieved only in a darkroom. By lowering the gray value of each pixel, you can make an image lighter. By reversing the gray values, you can convert it into a negative. Painting tools allow you to remove objects or add new ones. Cloning and texture tools allow you to reproduce a portion of an image elsewhere. Selection tools allow you to copy an object from one image and paste it into another.

Though image-editing programs vary widely in functionality, some features are common to all. These include painting tools, selection tools, image filters, and gray-scale editing functions. Gray-scale functions are especially useful in improving the ultimate quality of halftones produced on the imagesetter. They typically include brightness and contrast controls, histogram and equalization functions, and perhaps the most important of all, the gray-map—or gamma curve—editor.

The gray-map editor is a linear graph that shows how gray values in the original image (horizontal axis) correspond to values in the displayed image (vertical axis). In a normal image, the line runs diagonally from the lower left to upper right, showing a one-to-one correspondence between the two versions of the image. Pixels that were black in the original image are displayed as black, while pixels that were white are represented as white. But if you reverse the line, going from upper left to lower right, the pixels also become reversed. Black pixels in the original image display as white, and white pixels are displayed as black. The result is a negative.

By altering the shape and slope of the gray-map line, you can create interesting effects in an image. Increasing the slope of

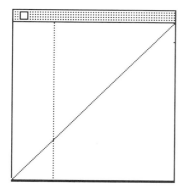

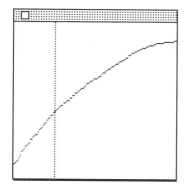

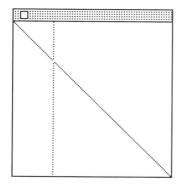

The gray-map editor is a linear graph that shows how gray values in the original image correspond to values in the displayed image. By altering the shape and slope of the gray-map line, you can create interesting effects.

the line, for example, raises the level of contrast by forcing most of the pixels toward the light and dark ends of the gray-scale spectrum. You can adjust brightness by raising or lowering the line. If you reverse the gray-level for selected ranges of grays, you can get an effect called solarization in which certain areas appear as negative images and others as positives. By limiting the number of gray levels you can get an effect called posterization, in which the halftone appears more like a line drawing than a photo.

In most cases, you will not want to perform such radical transformations. But subtle changes in the gray-map editor can go far in improving the quality of your digital halftones. These changes can correct distortions in gray values that occur at the input and output stages of the halftone production process. Many gray-scale scanners darken gray values in the midtone areas of the image. For example, a scanner may reproduce a 50-percent gray value in the original photograph as 80-percent gray or more. On the output side, many imagesetters show little variation in gray levels at either end of the gray-scale spectrum. A 10-percent gray shade looks white, and an 80- or 90-percent gray shade looks black. Some image-editing programs have automatic calibration functions to compensate for these distortions. But you can use the gray-map editor to perform a similar function. By giving the gray map a convex (bow-shaped) curve, you can lighten the gray values in midtone areas. By setting the darkest shades (also known as shadows) to 90 percent and the

A histogram is a graph showing how gray levels are distributed in an image. Each line represents a certain shade of gray; its length varies depending on how many pixels match the gray shade it represents.

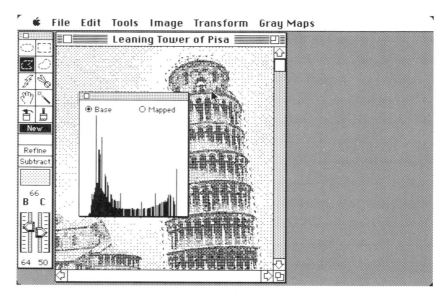

lightest shades (known as highlights) to about 10 percent, you can increase the range of gray shades the image can display.

Another useful gray-scale editing tool is the histogram, a graph consisting of vertical lines that show how gray levels are distributed in an image. Each line represents a certain shade of gray, from zero percent (white) on one side to 100 percent (black) on the other. Line lengths vary depending on how many pixels match the gray shade it represents. The best-looking images are generally those in which gray levels are distributed more or less evenly through the image. The number of light gray pixels, for example, should be roughly equal to the number of dark gray pixels. If the range of displayed gray levels is concentrated too much at the light or dark ends, detail can be lost.

The histogram itself does not allow you to alter gray values in an image. This is done with the gray-map editor or brightness and contrast controls. Many image-editing programs also include an Equalization function that explicitly redistributes gray shades in the image, spreading them more evenly across the graph. Be careful, however: gray values might be unevenly distributed due to the special nature of a particular image, and equalization could actually detract from image quality. Fortunately, most image-editing programs include an Undo function that allows you to return to the original distribution of gray shades.

Painting tools can also help enhance image quality by allowing you to fix scratches or perform other corrections. You can also use them to create original images and special effects. Unlike monochrome paint programs, which limit you to painting in black or white, image-editing programs allow you to paint in varying shades of gray selected from a palette or from the image itself. Cloning and texture tools allow you to click on a portion of an image and replicate it elsewhere. Click on a person's face, for example, and you can recreate the face—and everything around it—by painting in a different area of the image. Texture functions work in a similar manner, except they recreate the pattern immediately underneath the paintbrush rather than the area around it.

Almost all image-editing programs include functions that allow you to select a portion of an image on which you can then perform a variety of operations. These typically include a marquee tool for selecting rectangular areas and a lasso tool for objects with irregular shapes. Once an object is selected, you can move it, duplicate it, or cut and paste it to another area or a different image file. Some programs allow you to stretch or rotate selected image portions. You can also limit certain software operations to the area inside or outside the selected area. This is known as masking.

Some image-editing programs include a helpful "Paste-If" feature that allows you to control how cut-and-paste operations are performed. This allows you to specify a range of gray values that will be pasted over when creating a composite photograph. For example, if you want to paste a photo of clouds onto a photo showing a clear sky, you can specify the relatively light gray values of the sky as the only area of the image to be pasted on. When the clouds are dropped into the image, they cover the sky only, leaving other areas with different gray values unobscured.

Image filters allow you to alter the characteristics of pixels in selected portions of an image. These can be used to create special effects and to compensate for irregularities. Blur and soften filters, for example, reduce the contrast in an image, making it appear slightly out of focus. They are useful if the background in a photograph is so sharp that it diverts attention from objects in the foreground. Sharpening filters increase the contrast around edges in selected areas. Diffusion filters rearrange gray levels in small portions of an image, creating a special effect known as a mezzotint.

Edge-tracing filters provide even sharper contrast, convert-

Image filters allow you to alter the characteristics of an image. Here, we apply the edge tracing (left), blur (center), and sharpen filters.

ing the image into bit-mapped line art. However, images created in this manner should not be confused with object-oriented graphics created by programs like Adobe Illustrator or Corel Draw. To convert a bit-mapped halftone into an object-oriented image, you need to use an auto-tracing program, such as Adobe Streamline.

Using the Image

For many users, the final destination of a gray-scale image is a desktop publishing program. Almost all of these packages offer functions that allow you to crop or scale images. To scale an image means to reduce or enlarge it. To crop an image means to cut away a portion of it. This may be needed for aesthetic reasons if, for example, you want to draw attention to a particular object in a photograph. Cropping may also be required for design purposes. If you want to fit a horizontally oriented image into a vertical space, you'll need to crop away on the right or left. Of course, you can also do any necessary cropping or scaling when the image is scanned.

In addition to cropping and scaling features, some desktop publishing programs include image control functions that allow you to determine how scanned images are printed. These include brightness and contrast controls and simple gray-map editors. You can also set the dot shape, dot angle, and resolution of halftone screens.

The screen frequency you choose largely depends on your quality requirements and the type of paper stock on which you want to reproduce the image. If you plan to reproduce your pages on an absorbent paper stock like newsprint (the kind used in newspapers), maximum recommended screen frequency is 75 to 85 lpi. If you print on higher quality uncoated paper, maximum recommended screen frequency is about 100 lpi. Coated paper, used in most magazines, can handle halftones in the 100- to 150-lpi range.

Imagesetter manufacturers have found that certain screen frequencies produce the best halftone quality depending on the screen angle and imagesetter resolution. These recommended frequencies account for how the imagesetter builds the halftone cells. This doesn't mean that you'll get bad-looking halftones if you don't use these frequencies, but the recommendations do take full advantage of the imagesetter's imaging capabilities.

Producing the Image

Assuming you have made any necessary modifications to the image, printing it on a PostScript imagesetter is a relatively simple matter. One consideration is the output resolution to use. If you plan to produce an image with 256 levels of gray and a screen frequency of 100 lines or more, you probably need to go at the maximum resolution of 1693, 2540, or 3386 dpi depending on the imagesetter model you are using. To see why this is so, go back to our discussion above of the trade-off between resolution and gray levels. To compute the minimum resolution needed for various screen frequencies, take the square root of the number of gray levels in the image and multiply it by the desired screen frequency. In an image with 256 levels of gray, the square root is 16, which corresponds to the number of dots on each side of the halftone cell. Therefore, you need a resolution of at least 1600 dpi (16×100) if you want to produce a 100-line screen. If you want to produce a 150-line screen, you need a resolution of at least 2400 dpi (16×150).

Chapter Eight

Desktop Color Imaging

Perhaps no element of desktop publishing has stimulated as much discussion as desktop color. In recent years, the desktop publishing industry has made tremendous strides in hardware and software products for process color reproduction. But four-color process printing is an extremely complex matter, one that the graphic arts industry has been perfecting for quite some time. Not everyone believes that desktop publishing products will be able to replace all of the work now performed by traditional color printing systems.

Unlike other categories of desktop publishing, which are largely controlled by one type of software or hardware product, color desktop publishing requires the interaction of many systems—some computer-related, some printing-related. Manufacturers must not only provide powerful software tools for acquiring, correcting, and separating color photographs, they must also make sure that the quality requirements of color print customers are maintained in a reliable and consistent manner. This is the challenge now confronting manufacturers of color displays, color printers, color scanners, high-resolution imagesetters, and other related products.

In this chapter, we'll discuss the key elements in desktop color imaging. Readers should keep in mind that this area of desktop publishing is evolving even more quickly than the industry as a whole. We'll try to stick to the basic concepts of color reproduction, but we cannot avoid discussions of specific products. These products are ever-changing, and new ones with more powerful capabilities are continually coming to market.

So let us begin by exploring the way human beings perceive color.

Color Perception

Color begins with light. Visible light consists of electromagnetic energy that falls within a certain range of wavelengths. Stated less technically, it includes all the colors of the rainbow: red, orange, yellow, green, blue, indigo, and violet. Each color represents specific wavelengths within the overall spectrum of visible light.

When we look at something, what we are really seeing is reflected light. Objects that appear to be a certain color do so by absorbing some of the colors in the spectrum while reflecting others. An orange, for example, absorbs all colors but orange, which is reflected back to the eye. These reflected colors bounce off receptors in our eyes known as cones. Cones come in three varieties, one sensitive to red, one to blue, and one to green. By combining the input from the three kinds of cones, our brain gets its colorful view of the world.

Color Models

The basic colors that can be combined to form other colors are called primaries. Red, green, and blue are known as additive primaries: add together equal percentages of red, blue, and green light and you get white. Green and red in equal percentages produce yellow. Blue and green produce cyan; blue and red produce magenta. By varying the percentages of each additive primary, you can generate any color in the spectrum. Color viewed in this way is known as transmissive color, because it is produced by transmissions from luminous sources, such as TVs or computer monitors.

The colors produced by the union of the additive primaries—cyan, yellow, and magenta—are known as subtractive primaries. These are the colors used in printing inks. They are called subtractive primaries because they absorb all the colors of the spectrum except for those that are reflected back to the eye. Each subtractive primary represents two additive primaries—red, green, or blue—without the third. Again, the subtractive primaries can be combined in various percentages to produce almost any color. Because they are perceived as colors reflected back to the human eye, images produced on paper with these subtractive primaries are known as reflective copy.

RGB and CYM—Red, Green, Blue, and Cyan, Yellow, Magenta—represent two different color models, or ways of describing colors. CYM, as we have noted, is the model used in commercial printing and other applications where color is reflected back to the eye from a non-luminous source. The RGB

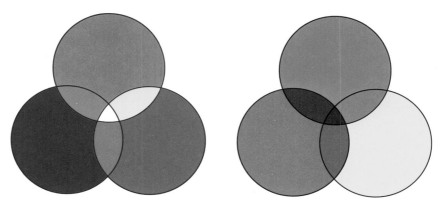

The additive primaries red, green, and blue (left) combine to make white. The subtractive primaries cyan, yellow, and magenta (right) combine to make black.

model is used in scanners, displays, and other products where color is transmitted from a luminous source.

A third model, known as HSL for Hue, Saturation, and Lightness, is also used for color measurement. Two similar models are HSV, for Hue, Saturation, and Value, and HSB, for Hue, Saturation, and Brightness. Hue represents the color itself, from red through violet. Saturation represents the purity of the color. For example, if a color includes a high degree of gray, its saturation is low. Saturation is high when grays are minimized. Lightness or value represents the brightness of the color. Again, almost any color shade can be represented as HSL, HSV, or HSB values. Some people find that these are the most intuitive forms of color description.

Effect of Lighting

We can see that light has much to do with our perception of color. A color photograph can look much different depending on whether you see it under candlelight in a darkened room or outside in bright sunlight. Graphics experts use the term "color temperature" to describe the degree of illumination in a particular environment. It is measured in Kelvin. Standard daylight has a color temperature of about 5000 Kelvin. An office illuminated by fluorescent light has a relatively cool color temperature of 4100 Kelvin. The standard Macintosh display has a color temperature of 9300 Kelvin. Some display products allow you to adjust the color temperature of a computer monitor so it can more accurately show color images.

Color perception is a complex process influenced by many variables. That's why it is such a challenge to produce good-looking color images, especially with desktop systems. Now we'll look at the two principal categories of color reproduction.

Spot Color Reproduction

The simplest and least expensive form of color reproduction is spot color. As its name implies, this is a single color applied to one or more elements on the page. For example, an ad in the local Yellow Pages might have the shop's name and phone number in red, and the rest of the information in black.

Producing spot color is relatively easy. The lithographer makes a printing plate for each color to be used in the ad. For example, the elements to be printed in red appear on one plate. The items to be printed in blue appear on a second plate. Items to be printed in black go on a third plate. On a single-color press, pages are then run through the press three times, one for each plate and ink color. If a four-color press is used, the pages are actually run through only once, but the basic principle is the same.

Preparing Copy

Print customers can prepare camera-ready color lithography in one of two ways. The easiest method is often to print the entire page in black and white, then use a tissue overlay to indicate the portions that should be printed in different colors. When making the spot color plate, the lithographer masks any area of the page that won't be printed in the extra color. The alternative is to produce three separate versions of the page (four if you add a second spot color). One, known as the composite page, includes all text and graphic elements to be printed. The second page includes only those elements to be printed in the spot color. The third page includes everything else. Each page, known more technically as an overlay, typically includes registration marks that allow for proper alignment.

PANTONE MATCHING SYSTEM®*

One tricky aspect of working with spot colors is identifying them. Suppose you want to produce a flyer with a headline in a particular shade of blue. How do you communicate that request to the lithographer without submitting a sample? One answer is found in the PANTONE MATCHING SYSTEM.

The PANTONE MATCHING SYSTEM is a set of standardized colors developed by a New Jersey-based company called Pantone, Inc. Pantone publishes a series of books showing hundreds of colors used in commercial lithography. They begin with nine basic colors, including three shades of red and two shades of blue. These colors are identified by name: PANTONE Warm Red, PANTONE Rubine Red, PANTONE Reflex Blue, and so on. Most of the remaining colors in the books are mixtures of these basic shades

*PANTONE MATCHING SYSTEM® is a registered trademark of Pantone, Inc.

The PANTONE MATCHING SYSTEM is a set of standardized colors used in commercial lithography. Many desktop color programs allow you to choose PANTONE values directly. (Note: Process color reproduction of PANTONE-identified colors may not match solid color standards. Use current PANTONE Reference Manuals for accurate color.)

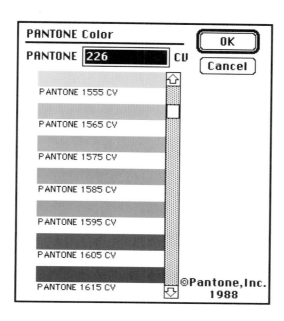

identified by a code number. For example, PANTONE 151 is a mixture of 12 parts PANTONE Yellow and four parts PANTONE Warm Red that combine into a shade of orange.

Pantone licenses its color-coding scheme to manufacturers of printing inks. If you specify a PANTONE code in your print job, a press operator can refer to the PANTONE Color Formula Guide 1000 for the ink mixture needed to produce the specified color and match it using ink from any licensee. The PANTONE Book also includes a selection of seven "Day-Glo" colors and seven metallic colors, including gold, bronze, copper, and silver.

PANTONE Color Publications are available at art supply stores for $30 to $195. Pantone publishes the guides on coated and uncoated stock to account for differences in how colors are seen on each type of paper. If you purchase one, be sure it is printed on the type of paper you intend to use for your color work. Pantone also recommends that the guides be replaced every year or so due to "uncontrollable pigment fading, varnish discoloration, and paper aging."

The PANTONE MATCHING SYSTEM is not the only way to specify spot colors. The four process colors, cyan, yellow, magenta, and black, can also be blended into spot colors. This is generally preferred when you have a lot of spot colors to apply, if your printer does not use the PANTONE MATCHING SYSTEM, or if you just don't want to purchase a color-matching guide. An alternative to the PANTONE MATCHING SYSTEM is the PANTONE Process

Color System which contains 3,006 chromatically arranged CMYK combinations. PANTONE is the dominant color matching system supported by most desktop publishing products.

Process Color Reproduction

Spot color reproduction is relatively straightforward and easy to master. Unfortunately, many printing jobs require a more demanding form of color reproduction known as process color. Process color is used to reproduce photographs and other complex images. It is also used as a substitute for the PANTONE MATCHING SYSTEM in process jobs that include spot color work. Pantone publishes CMYK equivalents to PANTONE MATCHING SYSTEM colors in the PANTONE Process Color Imaging Guide 1000.

In process color reproduction, images are broken down into four component colors: cyan, yellow, magenta, and black. We mentioned earlier that almost any color can be described as various shades of cyan, yellow, and magenta. However, these colors do not combine well when producing darker shades, especially black. For this reason, black is added as a fourth process color.

To produce a page using process color, the designer provides the lithographer with four pieces of film known as separations. The separations are one-color negatives, but each corresponds to one of the process colors: cyan, yellow, magenta, and black. The lithographer converts the separations into printing plates, and runs the pages through the press four times, once for each color. If everyone has done their job, the CMYK inks combine to reasonably reproduce the image. In many cases, a designer may add a fifth or sixth separation for an extra color that cannot be reproduced adequately using the CMYK system. This is often done when the job requires a metallic ink, such as gold or silver or strong, saturated colors.

Traditional Color Separations

Before the days of desktop publishing, separations for offset color lithography were produced largely by expensive prepress systems from companies like Crosfield, Scitex, and Hell (which is now a part of Linotype). Unlike microcomputer systems, which consist of standardized components from various vendors, color prepress systems are proprietary. This means that all components are manufactured by a single company and sold as a package.

The heart of most color prepress systems is a device known as a drum scanner. Unlike the scanners used in desktop publishing systems, a drum scanner can serve as both an input

As an image is converted into separations, the scanner operator can make a number of adjustments to improve its ultimate appearance. Simple adjustments include cropping and resizing, but an experienced operator can also sharpen blurry edges or make subtle adjustments in the percentages of each color. Because of imperfections and inconsistencies in color inks, some CYMK combinations do not produce an accurate reproduction of the original colors. By adjusting the color percentages, the scanner operator can correct these kinds of problems. This kind of color correction requires a lot of skill and experience.

Color Proofing

One important aspect of color reproduction is proofing. Color printing is tricky under the best of circumstances, and many customers want to see their pages before paying thousands of dollars for a commercial lithographer. Unfortunately, looking at four pieces of film is not going to give you a great idea of how your color image will look when it's printed. Because of this, several companies have devised methods for producing color proofs that provide a more-or-less accurate reproduction of the image. These systems include Du Pont's Cromalin® and 3M's Matchprint® and Color-Keys.

In addition to these proofing mechanisms, color designers and lithographers use devices known as densitometers and colorimeters to measure printed color. A densitometer, true to its name, measures the density of a color or gray shade. However, it does so in negative terms. For example, if the densitometer measures the density of blue as zero, 100 percent

3M's Matchprint (left) and Du Pont's Cromacheck (right) are two popular color proofing systems.

In addition to these proofing mechanisms, color designers and lithographers use devices known as densitometers and colorimeters to measure printed color. A densitometer, true to its name, measures the density of a color or gray shade. However, it does so in negative terms. For example, if the densitometer measures the density of blue as zero, 100 percent of the blue light is being reflected or transmitted back to the eye. Densitometers, unfortunately, are not always accurate in measuring colors as they are perceived by the eye. Colorimeters, a similar type of device, are more accurate in measuring color as it will be perceived.

Desktop Color

Many factors come into play when you try to produce color separations on a desktop publishing system. If you plan to work with color photographs, you need a scanner capable of capturing a color image with a high degree of fidelity. If you want to see your work accurately displayed on the screen, you need a properly calibrated color monitor. If you want high-quality film output, you need an imagesetter capable of precise registration and repeatability. But unless you have software capable of producing color separations, all that expensive hardware will come to naught.

In the past year or two, software developers have come a long way toward adding color separation capabilities to their packages. Whether you use an image-editing program, illustration software, or a desktop publishing package, chances are fair to good that your computer system can produce color separations. However, doing so can still be a rather complex undertaking. It's certainly a lot more complicated than selecting the "Print" command from the file menu and letting the pages rip from your laser printer.

The basic procedure for producing process color separations is actually pretty simple. We know that almost any color can be represented as a combination of three primary colors: cyan (a light blue), yellow, and magenta (a shade of red). By mixing these primaries in various percentages, you can produce almost any color visible to the human eye. Orange, for example, is mostly a combination of magenta and yellow. However, darker colors produced in this way tend to look muddy, so black is often added to improve appearance and reduce the amount of ink needed on press. Process color separations are thus known as

CYMK separations ("K" is used instead of "B" to represent black, probably to avoid confusion with blue).

When you produce color separations with a desktop publishing or graphics program, the separation software produces four versions of the original color image, one for each of the CYMK primaries. Each of these versions is stored on disk, usually as a PostScript file. A service bureau then produces four pieces of film, again one for each of the primary colors. This film is sent to the printer, who creates press plates for each of the separations. On a single-color press, pages are then run through the printing press four times, once for each plate, resulting in the final printed color image (on a four-color press, the pages are run through once, but ink is still laid down separately for each plate).

It sounds simple, but much can go wrong on the way to the printing press. For example, each separation generally consists of dots printed at different angles as determined by the color separation software. If the wrong dot angles are used, moire patterns are likely to result because the primary colors will not blend together properly. Some of this is beyond the control of your color separation software. For example, many of the older imagesetters suffer from poor repeatability, while newer models offer precise registration and new technology for producing accurate screen angles. However, a good software package can do much to enhance the quality of process color output.

A major debate is raging over the merits of desktop color systems in comparison with traditional prepress systems. On the plus side, desktop systems are much less expensive than traditional prepress equipment, even if you include the cost of an imagesetter. Traditional systems are priced as high as $1 million. A PostScript imagesetter for producing color separations can be had for well under $100,000. A Macintosh Quadra system with large-screen color display, 120-megabyte hard drive, eight megabytes of memory, and a full complement of software costs less than $20,000. Most desktop color publishers get along without their own imagesetters; they use a service bureau instead.

Desktop color also offers the best of two worlds. Programs like Aldus PageMaker and Xerox Ventura Publisher brought publishing capabilities to the masses by offering page production tools in easy-to-use packages. For the first time, users had complete control over the appearance of pages without the intervention of a graphic artist. Desktop color promises the same kind of freedom for color publishers.

Limitations of Desktop Color

Unfortunately, microcomputer-based color systems have their limitations, especially in the areas of performance and output quality. One problem is that color images consume large amounts of memory and disk space—a slide scanned at 4096-line resolution and 24 bits of color requires about 60 megabytes. This can strain the capabilities of even the most powerful microcomputers. PC-based color systems may be cheap compared to traditional systems, but they still require a lot of expensive horsepower to handle color data. A large-screen, 32-bit color display costs about $5000—and that doesn't include an accelerator or calibrator.

Another problem with desktop color systems is a lack of reliable proofing mechanisms. That $5000 color monitor can display a photograph, but the methods for generating an image on an electronic display—which uses additive colors—are much different than those for printing subtractive process colors. An image that looks good on the screen can appear to have distorted colors when printed. Color PostScript printers are even less reliable. Some service bureaus that do desktop color work offer traditional color proofing systems like 3M's Color-Keys or MatchPrints. These are much more reliable than other proofing methods, but are expensive and unwieldy.

Finally, there's the question of quality. Most publishers of magazines and other color publications have high quality requirements, and many believe that desktop systems cannot meet their demanding standards. Though a few magazine publishers produce their color pages with desktop software, the vast majority still rely on traditional color separation systems.

Does this make desktop color systems mere curiosities? Not at all. Just as desktop publishing systems brought typesetting capabilities to the masses, desktop color systems bring color capabilities to publishers previously limited to a world of black and white. Candidates for desktop color systems include small newspapers, catalog publishers, and packaging designers—users who were scared away from traditional color because of its cost and complexity.

The nice thing about desktop color is that the products are getting better all the time. Many desktop publishing programs can now produce process color separations, even of photographs. Color graphics packages allow users to manipulate and enhance color images. Color display products are getting faster and more reliable.

Standards

One distinction between desktop systems and traditional prepress is the use of standardized components. Traditional prepress systems, we have noted, are based on proprietary equipment that cannot be used in systems from other vendors. Desktop users, however, can purchase a computer, display, printer, software, and other products from different vendors and configure their own systems. Almost all output is produced using PostScript, the *de facto* standard for page description languages. Standard file formats like TIFF and EPS can be used with a wide range of programs in multiple hardware environments.

This ability to mix and match system components is one reason why desktop color is so much cheaper than traditional color. Vendors of proprietary systems essentially have a captive audience that must purchase all components from a single source, and they charge accordingly. In an open system, many different vendors compete to supply the system components. This, and the larger market for microcomputer products, results in lower prices.

But there is also a downside to open systems. In a proprietary system, the manufacturer can be sure that all components work smoothly together to produce consistent, high-quality output. But when systems include products from multiple vendors, achieving this consistency proves to be more difficult. A slide captured on one company's scanner might look different than the same image captured with a competing product. A photograph might appear to have too much red on a certain monitor when the problem is really in the display, not the picture. Images that appear too light on one imagesetter might be too dark on another.

Hardware and software developers are addressing these problems with new products that allow users to compensate for differences among the various components in a system. As the standards that govern desktop color production are refined and extended, hardware and software products will no doubt learn to better cooperate with one another.

The most important standard in the desktop color market is PostScript. As PostScript devices, imagesetters are vital components in color production. They perform the ultimate step in the process: producing the same kinds of color separations that a drum scanner would produce in a traditional prepress system. But users must be sure they have the right machine for the job. Early imagesetters—and their RIPs—were designed for monochrome output, and proved to have limitations as color machines. Newer models, such as the Linotronic 630 and the Agfa SelectSet 7000, have improved color output features.

One challenge for the color imagesetter is producing separations with a high degree of repeatability. This means that dots are correctly aligned from one separation to another. If the separations are out of registration, the CYMK colors will not mix properly and the image will probably be distorted. Poor repeatability can also cause problems with trapping, a spot color technique described later in this chapter. Dot repeatability of two one-thousandths of an inch or less is considered sufficient for color production.

The Tools of Desktop Color

Before we get to the imagesetter, we need to produce our color pages with a desktop publishing system. It should be apparent by now that the cute little PC that sits on your desk for simple word processing applications may not be sufficient for color work. It takes a powerful combination of hardware and software tools to meet the requirements for color production.

First, there is the computer itself. Most of the exciting new products for color production run on the Macintosh, though IBM-compatible computers are beginning to catch up. The bottom line is that you need plenty of horsepower, especially when doing process color work. It takes a lot of data to describe a color image, so the computer must be fast and able to work with large amounts of memory. It should also be expandable, since you may need to add a display controller, scanner board, or other add-on products.

In the Macintosh environment, almost all color work is done on the Macintosh II and Quadra series; earlier models are limited to monochrome display. In the IBM environment, computers based on the 80286, 80386, or 80486 microprocessors are preferred. The 386 and 486 chips are best, but 486 systems tend to be more expensive.

Whatever type of computer you use, you'll need plenty of memory to work with color images. The minimum configuration for the Macintosh is four megabytes, with eight megabytes being preferred for process color work. PC users can get by with two megabytes, but again, the more memory the better. As more sophisticated color software moves to the PC, memory requirements will no doubt rise.

As we have seen, color images consume large amounts of disk

space. One manufacturer of a color scanner recommends that users purchase a 600-megabyte hard drive to store scanned images. It may sound like a lot, but one slide scanned at maximum resolution can consume up to 60 megabytes. You don't have to go as far as ordering a 600-megabyte disk drive, but you do need sufficient storage space to work with color images. Depending on the kind of color work you plan to do, this could mean anything from a 65-megabyte drive on up.

For many users, the main storage medium—the hard disk— is less important than the media used to transport color images to a service bureau. Relatively small images can be stored on 3.5-inch diskettes with capacities ranging up to 1.44 mega- bytes. If an image file is too large to fit on a single diskette, the user can use a backup program to divide the file among multiple

Removable hard drives from companies like Iomega and SyQuest allow storage of large color files on removable disks.

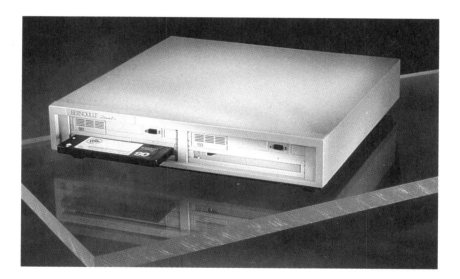

disks. File compression programs available in many public domain software libraries can also reduce file size.

In some cases, standard 3.5-inch diskettes are not enough. Many users working with especially large image files find themselves compelled to purchase removable hard drives. These products, from companies like Iomega and SyQuest, allow storage of large amounts of data—typically 44 to 90 mega- bytes—on removable disks. A user can easily copy all or most of the files involved in a color job and transport the disk to the service bureau. Unfortunately, there are few standards in the market for high-capacity removable disks. An Iomega disk, for example, will not work with a SyQuest drive. This means that before purchasing such a product, you should check with your service bureau to be sure they have a compatible drive.

Some companies have developed file compression products that can vastly reduce the size of color image files, making them easier to store and transmit. These products are sold in the form of software-only packages and hardware/software combinations. The latter are more expensive, but offer faster compression and decompression speeds.

The display is one of the most important elements in a desktop color system, especially given the absence of reliable proofing mechanisms. A good color display gives the user a reasonable idea of how an image will look when it is produced. Working with a bad display is like trying to paint a picture in the dark.

The primary distinction among color displays is the number of colors they can show for each dot (generally known as a "pixel") on the screen. This number is generally referred to in terms of "bits per pixel." A bit is the primary unit of data in a computer system. It can have one of two values: zero or one. A number described with 8 bits of data can have any one of 256 values. A number described with 24 bits of data can have any one of 16.8 million values. Each of these values can be used to represent a gray or color tint. An 8-bit image contains 256 colors or gray shades; a 24-bit image contains 16.8 million colors.

Many color monitors are limited to displaying eight bits, or 256 individual colors. This may sound like a lot, but images viewed on an eight-bit display tend to have a grainy, unrealistic appearance. Costlier monitors have 32-bit capability. In this case, the display can show 8 bits, or 256 shades, for each of the three primary additive colors—red, green, and blue—with 8 bits left over for other data. These monitors can show images that appear as realistic as a color photograph. Theoretically, a 32-bit display can show 16.8 million colors. In reality, few monitors can actually display that many colors because they don't have 16.8 million pixels on the screen.

All displays, color or monochrome, conform to certain standards. On the Macintosh, that standard is known as QuickDraw, which is Apple's name for the software that allows the computer to show images on the screen. Most color QuickDraw displays use 8 bits of color, but 32-bit QuickDraw is used in many large-screen color monitors.

The most popular color display standards in the IBM-compatible environment are CGA, EGA, and VGA. VGA, the most recent standard, is preferred for most color production work, especially with photographs. Standard VGA offers a choice of 320 by 200 pixel resolution and 64 colors, or 640 by 480 and 16 colors. Users can boost resolution and bit depth by using Super VGA displays or the 8514/A extension for VGA. CGA, the oldest standard, is seriously limited in its resolution and the number of colors that can be displayed, and should be avoided.

Several companies manufacture products that enhance the use of color displays for publishing work. These include graphics accelerators and calibrators. Graphics accelerators are boards that speed up the display of color images, and are especially useful with 24- and 32-bit monitors. Calibrators are hardware/ software products that adjust the way a monitor projects colors to account for lighting conditions and changes in the monitor itself.

One such product, the PrecisionColor Calibrator from Radius, includes a sensing device that attaches to the monitor along with utility software that performs the calibration. In addition to altering the mix of RGB color components, the calibration system can adjust the display's color temperature to simulate various proofing situations. For example, you can set the temperature at 5000 Kelvin, which is the industry standard for proofing color prints.

Another feature is the ability to account for the monitor's

The PrecisionColor Calibrator from Radius includes a sensing device that attaches to the monitor along with utility software that performs calibration.

gamma distortion. A gamma curve is a graph that compares the brightness of an image stored in the computer with the same image as it is displayed. Ideally, the graph should show a diagonal line representing a one-to-one correspondence: each pixel in the displayed image should have the same brightness as the stored image. But most displays have a slightly distorted gamma curve, which tends to make images look slightly darker or lighter than they should. The PrecisionColor Calibrator can adjust the curve to ensure accurate image display.

Some software products offer a crude but inexpensive form of display calibration that depends on the human eye. In Fractal Design's ColorStudio, for example, the manual includes a color photograph of men in a sailboat. When the program is launched, it displays the photograph on the computer screen. A user can then adjust the monitor's brightness and contrast to get the closest possible match between the printed and displayed versions of the photo. Other programs use a color ramp—a bar displaying a wide range of colors—in place of a photograph.

Proofing represents one of the most difficult aspects of desktop color. Aside from the color display, users have little opportunity to see how their pages will look when printed. One product that does allow a form of proofing is the color PostScript printer. We'll look at color printers in more detail in Chapter Nine.

A more reliable proofing alternative is provided by traditional proofing systems, such as 3M's Color-Keys and Matchprints. These systems use a variety of methods to produce realistic proofs from color separations generated on the imagesetter. However, they are expensive and unwieldy. The Matchprint system, for example, costs about $75,000. It uses heat lamination technology to produce the proofs, consuming large amounts of electricity and requiring more than an hour to warm up. Another disadvantage is that you cannot tell how your image will look until it has already been produced as separations on the imagesetter.

Hardware, of course, only tells half the story when it comes to desktop color. New software packages have been essential to advances in digital color applications. In some cases, developers have added color production capabilities to existing programs. Other developers have introduced products that specifically address one or more aspects of color input, design, or production.

Software used in color production falls into many categories. Scanner software is used with the scanner to capture images and store them in one of several standard file formats. Color editing software allows the user to retouch, combine, and adjust color images to improve their appearance or create special effects. Color illustration software uses an object-oriented approach to color design as opposed to the bit-mapped approach in color editing programs. Color-oriented desktop publishing software can incorporate color images produced with other programs, as well as applying colors to text and graphics created within the package. Color separation software is used to produce process color separations from files created by desktop publishing or graphics programs. Many software packages combine these functions.

Producing desktop color involves more than a single process and a single software package.

Color Image-Editing Software

Once an image is scanned, its next destination is usually a color image-editing package, such as Adobe Photoshop or Fractal Design's ColorStudio on the Mac or Photostyler, Picture Publisher, or PhotoFinish on the PC. These programs allow you to perform a wide range of editing, retouching, and image manipulation functions. In many ways, they are similar to gray-scale image-editing programs like Letraset's ImageStudio and Silicon Beach Software's Digital Darkroom. However, instead of manipulating gray shades, these programs allow you to work with each of the primary colors in the image. Although each package has its own unique features, a number of general functions are common to all.

Painting tools in color image-editing programs are similar to those found in their gray-scale counterparts. A paintbrush tool is used to retouch portions of an image or to add special effects. A paint bucket tool, as its name implies, allows you to pour a color or pattern into a section of an image. Spray paint tools provide an airbrush effect. Other common tools include a "pencil" for adding and deleting individual dots; a "teardrop" for softening edges; and a "fingerpaint" tool that allows you to smudge colors in the image.

Most image-editing programs provide a high degree of control over how these tools are employed. For example, you can select a color from a portion of an image by clicking on it. Cloning functions, like those in gray-scale image-editing programs, allow you to click on a portion of an image and replicate it elsewhere. Texture functions work in a similar manner, except they recreate the pattern immediately underneath the paintbrush rather than the area around it.

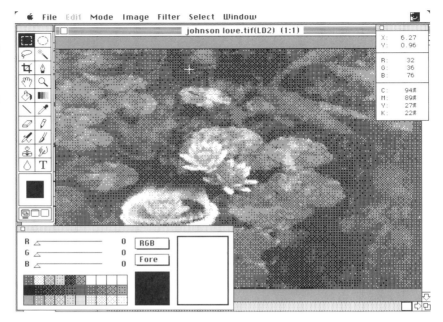

Color image-editing programs like Photoshop allow you to perform a wide range of editing, retouching, and image manipulation functions.

Selection tools allow you to select a portion of an image on which you can then perform a variety of operations. These typically include a marquee tool for selecting rectangular areas and a lasso tool for objects with irregular shapes. More advanced selection tools, such as the magic wand in Adobe Photoshop, allow you to click inside an irregular object to select it automatically. The program performs this feat by seeking pixels with similar color values, so it works best when there is a strong contrast between the object and surrounding areas.

Once an object is selected, you can move it, duplicate it, or cut-and-paste it to another area or a different image file. Some programs allow you to stretch or rotate selected image portions. You can also limit certain software operations to the area inside or outside the selected area. This is known as masking.

In addition to its standard selection tools, Fractal Design's ColorStudio has an especially powerful masking function. The program uses two "layers"—a color layer for image display and a masking layer that acts as a stencil. Most functions that can be used in the color layer can also be used in the masking layer. For example, you cut-and-paste the image of a tree onto the mask to create a cookie cutter effect. Any paint applied to the mask only shows through where the tree has been pasted. By adding gray shades to the masking layer, you can create a screen that filters out some of the paint, producing a tint effect.

Filters are special effects that manipulate the color values in

Aldus PhotoStyler is a color image-editing program that runs under Microsoft Windows.

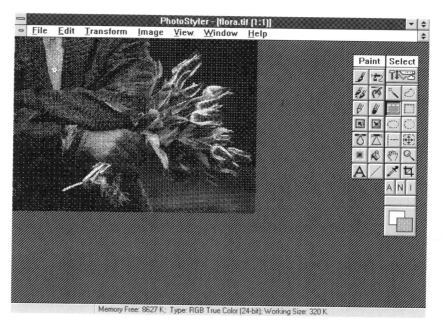

an image. In most cases, you can perform the filter operation on the entire image or selected portions. Common filters include blurring, sharpening, edge tracing, and despeckling, which removes random pixels from the image. Sometimes these are used to create special effects. In other cases they are used to improve the general appearance of the image.

Using the program's cut-and-paste features, you can create images composed of sections from other images. For example, you may want to add clouds to a blue sky in a landscape scene. To do this, you need two images, one of the clouds and one of the landscape. Using selection tools, you can select the clouds from the first image, copy them to the program's clipboard, then paste them into the second image. Most image-editing programs provide some sort of blending function so that the first image blends smoothly into the second one.

Color adjustment functions allow you to change the mix or intensity of colors or replace one color with another. There are several reasons why you may want to do this: to improve the general appearance of an image, to create certain kinds of special effects, or for calibration purposes.

Earlier, we discussed a function in many image-editing programs known as the gray-map editor. Color mapping functions work in a similar manner, except that instead of working with shades of gray, we are working with shades of red, green, and blue, and ultimately the CYMK colors as well.

In some programs this is handled by means of a graph, similar to the gray-map editor, that shows the relationship between pixels in the original image and pixels in the display. The difference is that there is one graph for each color, plus a fourth graph that represents the entire image. By adjusting the transfer lines on these graphs, you can brighten or darken an image, or increase or decrease its contrast. A slightly curved transfer line can create a smoother transition among colors than a straight diagonal line. A concave transfer line—one that dips down in the middle—emphasizes the light (highlight) and dark (shadow) areas of the image while de-emphasizing the mid-tones. A convex line—one that curves up in the middle— emphasizes the mid-tones at the expense of highlights and shadows.

In addition to its remapping functions, Adobe Photoshop can adjust color balance by means of sliding controls for each color. You can choose to add or subtract the amounts of cyan, magenta, or blue in the shadow, midtone, or highlight regions of the image. You can also adjust hue and saturation using similar controls.

Finally, many color editing programs can produce CYMK color separations. Simply stated, this means creating four PostScript files—one each for cyan, yellow, magenta, and black— and having them produced on film media on a Linotronic imagesetter. But the reality is far from simple, as the software must often make adjustments to the image file to ensure the best possible output results. Some software developers have automated this process by adding what are known as "lookup tables" for each output device to their programs. The lookup table contains information about the output characteristics of popular printers and imagesetters. The software uses the lookup table to make minor modifications to the image that will improve its appearance on that particular output device.

Color Desktop Publishing Software

Many desktop publishing packages, including Aldus PageMaker, QuarkXPress, and DesignStudio, have built-in functions for producing spot or process color. In most cases, colors can be applied to headlines, rules, boxes, and other page elements. They can be specified as combinations of process colors, or as colors from the Pantone Matching System. You can also import color images from illustration or image-editing programs.

Your ability to produce color depends on whether you want

spot color separations or separations of color photographs. Remember that spot color can be produced in one of two ways: as a separate overlay for each of the spot colors, or as process color separations that create spot colors as combinations of cyan, yellow, magenta, and black.

The leading color separation programs on the Macintosh include Aldus PrePrint, which works with PageMaker; DesignStudio Separator, which works with DesignStudio; and SpectreSeps QX, a separation package from Pre-Press Technologies that works with QuarkXPress. Adobe sells a program called Adobe Separator that works with Illustrator files. In the Windows environment, Ventura Software offers two packages, Ventura Separator and Ventura ColorPro, which perform separation functions.

These packages work with files that have already been created by the publishing software. With PrePrint, for example, the process begins with a PageMaker document that includes color TIFF images. The first step is to save the publication in a format known as OPI, short for "Open Prepress Interface." This is a special kind of file designed for use with color separation programs. Using PrePrint, you open the OPI file and produce the separations. These separations can be printed directly to the output device, or produced as EPSF files. PrePrint also includes functions that allow you to enhance or adjust the image.

Using a color separation program like Aldus Preprint, you can produce color separations from desktop publishing files.

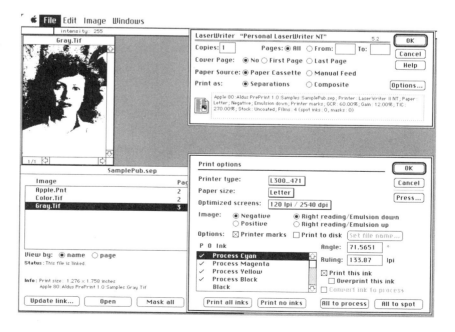

Quality Control

The final step in the color publishing process is to produce four separations, one each for cyan, yellow, magenta, and black, on a high-resolution imagesetter. Each separation will include a halftone of the color image in which the dots are printed at different angles. The angle of the dots is generally determined by the color separation software. If the wrong dot angles are used, moire patterns are likely to result because the primary colors will not blend together properly.

Before going to the time and expense of producing color separations, it is important that users communicate with representatives from the service bureau or print shop.

Registration Factors

These factors can get pretty complex. For example, even the best printing press will have difficulty producing pages with perfect registration. In other words, the colors can shift slightly from one separation to the next. One way to compensate for this, at least in spot color production, is by using a method called trapping. There are two types of traps: spreads and chokes. In a spread, areas printed in a light color are permitted to spread into areas printed in a dark color. This eliminates any gap that might appear between the two areas. In a choke, dark areas are permitted to spread slightly into light areas, again eliminating any gaps. Some color separation packages allow you to determine the degree of trapping when you produce the CYMK overlays. This form of trapping should not be confused with "ink trapping," an unrelated printing phenomenon in which inks mix improperly and produce distorted colors.

Dot Gain

Another problem that occurs on the printing press is dot gain. When ink is laid on the paper, it tends to spread slightly, which results in an enlarged dot. The degree of dot gain depends on the type of ink and paper used in the printing process, as well as the condition of the printing press. For example, uncoated paper stocks generally produce more dot gain than coated stocks. Some color editing programs, such as Adobe Photoshop, offer features that allow you to compensate for dot gain. Again, it is important for users to communicate with their print shop to find out what kind of dot gain can be expected and how to compensate for it. In general, if the degree of dot gain is high, the density of the dots on the separations should be reduced.

Undercolor Removal

In some cases, it may be advisable to perform an operation known as undercolor removal to adjust the mixture of CYMK primaries on the printed page. This technique takes advantage of the black color component to reduce the total amount of ink needed to print a page. We mentioned earlier that a mixture of 100-percent cyan, yellow, and magenta produces solid black. Equal mixtures of the three primaries in lighter densities produce gray. Undercolor removal is the process of replacing "neutral color areas"—those with equal percentages of cyan, yellow, and magenta—with the appropriate shade of gray. A similar technique known as gray component replacement uses black ink to adjust the overall density of the image.

Some color-oriented graphics programs offer a form of undercolor removal as part of their output functions. For example, in Adobe Photoshop, you can specify one of five degrees of black replacement—none, light, medium, heavy, and maximum—or a custom amount. To use this feature correctly, it is important to communicate with your printer to learn about the density of the inks they use on press.

In addition to reducing the amount of ink used on press, undercolor removal also ensures greater consistency if you have to produce the same publication on multiple printing presses. Printers generally find it easier to measure and control blacks and grays than mixtures of cyan, yellow, and magenta. By replacing CYM components with a single gray component, you can make it easier to control the density of the image. However, there are times when undercolor removal is not advised. It can be difficult to change the balance of CYM primaries after undercolor removal is performed. If a client decides at the last minute to change the color balance, it could lead to costly delays. Also, light gray screens composed of the CYM color components often look smoother than screens composed entirely of black dots.

Electronic publishing systems make it a lot easier to produce color separations, but it is still a lot more than a point-and-click process. Producing good-looking color pages with graphics or desktop publishing software requires effective interaction among all the elements in the system. It also requires communication among the user, service bureau, and print shop. Some day, color pages will be as easy to produce as monochrome pages are now. That day has not yet arrived, but current packages have taken a giant step toward allowing production of color separations from the desktop.

Chapter Nine

Producing Output

Desktop publishing programs allow users to create documents within the digital environment of a computer system. But at some point, we need to bring those documents into the real world. In other words, our pages must be printed. "Printing" has a double meaning here. It refers to the process of generating pages on a laser printer or imagesetter, but also applies to reproducing those pages through photocopying or offset lithography. In this chapter, we will discuss the first meaning of the word.

Users have many alternatives when it comes to producing pages. Some produce final output on a laser printer. Others use laser printers to generate proofing copies of pages that are later produced on a high-resolution imagesetter. Users who plan to produce color output may first turn to a color PostScript printer for comps and proofs, and then to an imagesetter or high-end prepress system for CYMK separations.

A user's output strategy is determined by what they plan to do with the document. If the page is to be printed in black and white and quality requirements are modest, a laser printer will probably suffice. If quality requirements are high, users may need access to a service bureau's imagesetting equipment. An imagesetter or color prepress system is pretty much required if the user wants to produce high-quality color output.

It is easy to see that hardware plays an important part in this discussion. We'll begin with a look at the page description languages that drive most of the output devices used in desktop publishing. Then we'll look at the various hardware options available to publishing users.

Page Description Languages

When electronic publishing first became a major graphics application in the mid-1980s, one of the key driving forces was the page description language (PDL). Like other computer programming languages, PDLs could perform powerful mathematical and graphical operations. But unlike languages such as BASIC or FORTRAN, PDLs run on output devices such as laser printers, imagesetters, or displays. And fortunately for end-users, they don't have to write the programs that produce PDL output. That task is performed by application software, such as word processors and page layout programs.

PostScript

In the last few years, Adobe Systems' PostScript has become the most important output standard for developers of high-quality graphics and publishing software. Desktop publishing

One advantage of PostScript is device independence: a page produced with a program that supports PostScript can be generated with little or no modification on any PostScript printer or imagesetter.

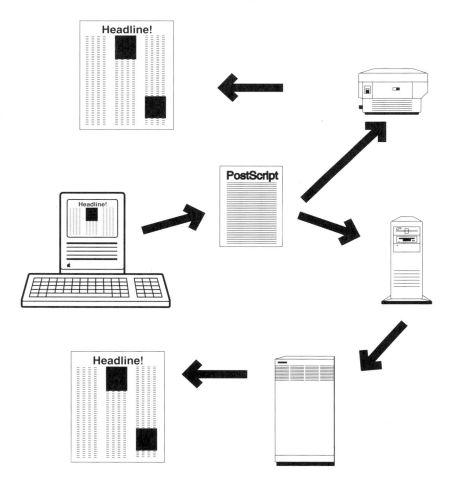

users have immediate access to a wide variety of programs running on many different computers that support PostScript. Users can be assured not only that a wide variety of programs will be available but, more important, that those programs will perform at their best when a PostScript output device is used. Most of this software can support non-PostScript printers, but in many cases the program's full range of features will not be available to users without PostScript devices.

PostScript users have access to the finest quality fonts available for their machines. These include fonts from Linotype (which also licenses them to Adobe), Bitstream, URW, and others. While the actual quality of type produced on a printer or imagesetter depends heavily on the resolution of that device, PostScript ensures that font quality will be the best possible at that resolution. For example, if a laser printer has a resolution of 300 dpi, PostScript cannot image fonts at a resolution greater than 300 dpi. But it can optimize the placement and arrangement of dots on the page so that each character in each font is true to the original typeface design and as readable as possible.

Another benefit is the wide variety of typefaces and point sizes available to PostScript users. Unlike other laser printers and typesetters, PostScript devices need store only one representation of each typeface. Any point size can be derived from this compact and precise mathematical representation. This saves the user and output device a tremendous amount of memory compared to the devices that force users to store, and many times purchase, a separate version of each typeface in each point size.

PostScript users also enjoy the benefit of device independence. This means that a page or publication produced with a program that supports PostScript can be generated with little or no modification on any PostScript printer or imagesetter. No matter what the resolution of that output device, the page can be produced at the maximum resolution and with the maximum quality.

For all its power, PostScript proved to have some limitations, especially in the area of color. Its lack of a device-independent color space forced hardware and software developers to implement their own awkward mechanisms for ensuring high-fidelity color output. Its halftoning algorithms, though adequate for monochrome images, sometimes produced moire patterns and other problems in color halftones. And its performance often suffered when producing color output, even on devices equipped with the latest high-speed processors.

Adobe addressed some of these problems by introducing several extensions to the basic PDL in the years following its release. Color extensions introduced in 1988 included support for the CYMK color model in addition to RGB and HSB, along with a *color image* operator for rendering color images. However, these features were implemented only in certain output devices. Other extensions included Display PostScript—a version of the language for screen display—and a "composite font" feature that allowed creation of large character sets.

PostScript Level 2

PostScript Level 2, announced by Adobe Systems in 1990, is the first comprehensive upgrade to the page description language. It consolidates the many extensions made to PostScript since its original introduction and adds many new functions on top of these. Though it is upwardly compatible with existing PostScript devices, it has enough new features that many hardware and software developers may find it necessary to completely rework their products.

Many of the new features are aimed at color users. The new PDL supports several device-independent color spaces based on CIE 1931(XYZ)-space, a standard method for describing color that is based on human visual perception. In theory, the color space acts as a reference point to ensure consistent color output on different printers and imagesetters.

In addition to these color spaces, PostScript Level 2 includes improved algorithms for producing halftones. Some of the improvements apply to all halftones, while others are specific to color images. The general improvements include faster performance and the ability to specify a much wider range of halftone screen angles and frequencies. Halftone screens allow digital output devices such as laser printers and imagesetters to approximate the full range of tonal values in a photograph using patterns of dots. The frequency, or spacing, and angle of dot placement determine the perceived quality of a halftone image.

The original PostScript, in contrast, was limited to a relatively narrow set of angle and frequency combinations. The color-specific improvements include the ability to generate screen angles accurate to 0.05 degrees or better. This is especially important when producing color separations, since the dots must be precisely angled to avoid moire patterns. Some developers of PostScript imagesetters, notably Linotype-Hell and Agfa, have introduced their own halftone screening technologies that work in conjunction with PostScript.

PostScript Level 2 also offers improved font-rendering functions. The composite font function, first introduced as a PostScript extension, provides for the incorporation of multiple fonts into a single character set. This is especially useful for foreign languages that use non-Roman character sets.

The new PDL also includes a variety of built-in compression/decompression filters, including CCITT Group II and IV for monochrome images, run-length encoding for monochrome and gray-scale, LZW for text, and DCT, a JPEG-compatible filter for color images. JPEG, short for Joint Photographic Experts Group, is a proposed international standard for image compression and decompression that has been endorsed by many hardware and software developers.

One other new feature that deserves mention is Level 2's support for forms generation. Users can define a base form containing text and graphic elements that can be repeated from page to page. Because the base form is stored in a memory or disk cache, the software will only need to generate the information that changes from page to page. As a result, Level 2 allows for much faster performance for any application that uses repeating page elements. In this context, a "form" can be a company logo, letterhead, or repeating slide background in addition to a traditional business form.

In addition to PostScript Level 2, Adobe introduced a new font-rendering technology called Multiple Masters that addresses some of the most serious font-handling problems in the original PostScript. In a nutshell, Multiple Masters technology allows users to generate a wide range of character widths, weights, sizes, and styles from a single set of typeface outlines. The technology offers users a much greater degree of flexibility in specifying typefaces. It also allows for improved document portability. Currently, if you specify a font that is not present in a PostScript output device, the printer or imagesetter will substitute a different typeface, usually with poor results. With Multiple Master technology, the system can produce a typeface that more closely approximates the original.

Alternatives to PostScript

Though PostScript is by far the most popular output standard in the desktop publishing market, some alternatives are available. In most cases, these alternatives offer a less expensive option for publishing users who balk at the relatively high cost of PostScript output devices. But as with all low-cost alternatives, there are also trade-offs in terms of quality, performance, convenience, and compatibility.

PostScript's popularity has led a number of companies to develop PostScript-compatible languages, popularly known as PostScript clones. These languages are usually packaged with interpreters and controllers that drive laser printers or imagesetters. In theory, they can interpret all PostScript commands, generating output that is identical to what a true PostScript device would produce.

PostScript clones are sold in several forms. The least expensive are software-only products that can print PostScript files on a non-PostScript printer. They tend to be very slow and usually require some form of extra memory on the computer or in the printer. Other clones are found on controllers installed in the computer or built into the printer itself. Still others are sold as cartridges that plug into the printer.

One PostScript clone that has received much attention is TrueImage, which was developed by Microsoft. Microsoft's dominant position in the computer software market gave TrueImage instant credibility, and several developers of laser printers have turned to it as a low-cost alternative to PostScript. However, Microsoft has backed away from its original goal of establishing TrueImage as the page description standard in the publishing market, and sees the PDL largely as an alternative means of providing output from the Windows environment.

Some inexpensive laser and inkjet printers use a language called QuickDraw instead of PostScript to generate pages. QuickDraw is a set of commands used by Apple's Macintosh to draw images on the screen. QuickDraw laser printers adapt these commands to draw 300-dpi images on the page. Though much less expensive than PostScript printers, QuickDraw printers are not recommended for production of graphics-intensive documents, especially those containing halftones.

Another alternative is Hewlett-Packard's PCL 5, which offers scalable typefaces in Agfa's Intellifont format. However, it lacks many of the other capabilities that distinguish PostScript, such as device independence and sophisticated imaging features. PCL 5 is found in HP's LaserJet Series III printers, which also offer PostScript output as an extra-cost option.

Some laser printer manufacturers offer products compatible with Hewlett-Packard's older LaserJet Series II, which does not offer scalable fonts. However, these printers can produce scalable typefaces if the user has installed Adobe Type Manager or a similar scalable typeface product like Bitstream's FaceLift. They can also produce PostScript-compatible output when used in conjunction with one of the PostScript clone products described above.

Laser Printers

The laser printer represents one of the most important elements in a desktop publishing system. It was Apple's LaserWriter, in combination with the Macintosh and publishing software, that created the desktop publishing boom to begin with. Even if users plan to produce most of their output on a high-resolution imagesetter, laser printers serve as an important method of proofing pages and producing comps.

Laser printers have come a long way since Hewlett-Packard introduced its LaserJet in 1984. That machine provided the same 300-dpi resolution as later printers, but offered a limited choice of typefaces and could render a full page of graphics at only 75 dpi. A year later, Apple Computer released the LaserWriter, a $7000 printer based on the PostScript page

The Apple LaserWriter was the first popular PostScript printer on the market.

description language. This device represented a quantum leap over the LaserJet in many ways, even though it was based on the same laser engine from Canon. Its 1 Mb of memory was sufficient to render full-page, 300-dpi graphics, and it was equipped with an interface allowing easy connection to a local area network. But its real advantage was the presence of

PostScript, which permitted tremendous flexibility in the use of type and graphics.

Most laser printers use a technology similar to that found in office copiers. Within the printer "engine" that provides the guts of the machine, a laser heats a rotating drum or belt, producing marks where toner should go. Once the drum is heated, it fuses toner to the paper, creating recognizable letters, numbers, and symbols. Another important element in the laser printer is the controller, which receives output from the computer system and converts it into instructions that drive the laser. In most PostScript printers, the controller is where the page description software resides. The controller also includes memory, which is used to store an image of the page before it is printed along with any typefaces resident in the printer or downloaded from the computer. In some cases, the controller can also be connected to a hard disk, which is used to store extra typefaces.

To communicate with the computer, a laser printer or other output device must have one or more of several standard interfaces. In the IBM environment, the two most popular interfaces are known as Centronic parallel and RS-232 serial. In the Macintosh environment, the most popular interface is AppleTalk. Because AppleTalk is designed to work within a local-area network, a single laser printer can be used in conjunction with any computer on the LAN. Some laser printers with high output speeds and especially durable designs are intended for use on large local-area networks. These "departmental" laser printers typically include interfaces for popular LAN standards like Ethernet and offer duty cycles as high as 70,000 pages per month.

High-Resolution Plain-Paper Printers

Though most laser printers offer 300-dpi output, many manufacturers offer printers that far exceed this resolution. Many users have found that they can produce text and simple line art that are virtually indistinguishable from the output of imagesetters that cost $30,000 or more. Some manufacturers go as far as to call their products "plain-paper typesetters." Imagesetters still have a big edge when producing halftones, but even in this area, plain-paper output devices are far superior to conventional 300-dpi laser printers.

High-resolution plain-paper printers fall into three categories. At the high end of the price/performance scale are printers that use laser engines designed for output resolutions of 600 dpi or more. The second category includes printers based on the Canon SX engine that use proprietary controller technology to boost resolution beyond the engine's 400-dpi limit. The third category includes upgrade kits for standard 300-dpi laser printers that increase their resolution to as much as 1000 dpi.

"True" high-resolution printers—those with engines designed for high-resolution output—generally cost $10,000 or more. Some of the major manufacturers in this category include Varityper, Printware, Hitachi, and Copal. Their resolution ranges from 600 to 1200 dpi. Some of these printers can produce tabloid-sized pages in addition to high-resolution output. Printware offers a version of its high-resolution printer that can produce output directly on plates.

High-resolution printers based on the Canon SX use proprietary software and controller hardware to alter the way the engine produces pages, pushing the resolution past its 400-dpi maximum (the SX is the same engine used in laser printers from Apple and Hewlett-Packard, though these manufacturers at first limited their resolution to a base of 300 dpi). Leading manufacturers in this category include LaserMaster, NewGen Systems, and more recently, QMS. Apple and Hewlett-Packard have introduced SX-based printers that use proprietary technology to increase the resolution of text and line art to the equivalent of 600 dots per inch. Apple also offers a technology

A 300-dpi printer produces jagged edges, while a 600-dpi product tends to produce smoother curves.

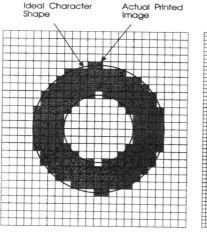

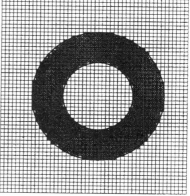

300 dpi x 300 dpi

Note jagged edges on curves that should be smooth.

600 dpi x 600 dpi

Higher resolution yields smoother curves and more accurate stroke widths. The result is improved text quality.

called PhotoGrade that improves the appearance of printed halftones. A LaserWriter printer equipped with PhotoGrade can produce halftones with screen frequencies of more than 100 lines and 73 levels of gray. This compares with 53-line screen frequencies and 33 levels of gray for an unenhanced 300-dpi printer engine.

The third category consists of printer controllers that upgrade existing printers to high-resolution capability. In a sense, these products allow users to add high-resolution output to their printers in the same way that developers have increased the resolution of the SX. The pioneer is this category was DP-Tek, whose TruePoint controller offers 600-dpi resolution. Other manufacturers include LaserMaster and XLI Corp. Many of these companies combine their controller with software that provides PostScript-compatible output.

Some manufacturers of high-resolution laser printers have made a lot of noise about how their products will make PostScript imagesetters obsolete. However, they are no match for even the most modest imagesetter when it comes to producing halftones. LaserMaster, for example, claims 1000 by 1000 dpi resolution for text, but only 400 by 1000 dpi for images. This translates into very limited screen frequencies because of the dithering process used to produce digital halftones. Another limitation is the medium itself. Plain paper does not hold dots as well as photographic media, especially film.

Inkjet Printers

One low-cost alternative to the laser printer is the inkjet printer. These products offer resolution of 300 dpi or more and can do a reasonable job of producing many kinds of output. However, 300-dpi resolution on an inkjet printer is not quite the same as 300-dpi laser output. A laser printer uses dry toner that is fused into the paper, while an inkjet printer uses a special kind of quick-drying ink. This ink tends to spread slightly when it contacts the paper, and also tends to bleed through the paper in areas of solid black. Inkjet printers are also relatively slow. However, with prices of $600 or less, they have appeal for cost-conscious users who are not deterred by their quality trade-offs.

Hewlett-Packard, with its DeskJet for the PC and DeskWriter for the Macintosh, was a pioneer in this area. Canon also offers an inkjet printer called the "BubbleJet," a version of which Apple offers as the StyleWriter. The DeskWriter and StyleWriter both use Apple's QuickDraw as their imaging language.

Citizen America offers the PM48 Notebook Printer, which

measures 2 inches high, 3.5 inches deep, and 11.5 inches wide. Though it uses an electrostatic process instead of inkjet technology, output quality is similar to what an inkjet device can produce. Its target market is laptop users who need laser-quality output on the road.

Color Printers

High-resolution (300 dpi or more) color printers are useful to service bureaus, publishers, and graphic designers who need an inexpensive means of proofing or comping color pages. They cannot produce color separations, but they provide a quick way for publishers to generate proofs of pages that will eventually be produced on a PostScript imagesetter or color separation system. They use one of several technologies, with thermal-transfer, inkjet, and dye sublimation the most common.

Thermal-Transfer Printers

In a thermal-transfer engine, a print head melts tiny dots of plastic or wax into the paper. The plastic or wax is stored on sheets or ribbons, contained in a cartridge, that scroll through the printer in much the same way that film moves through a

The QMS ColorScript is a 300-dpi color printer that uses thermal-transfer technology.

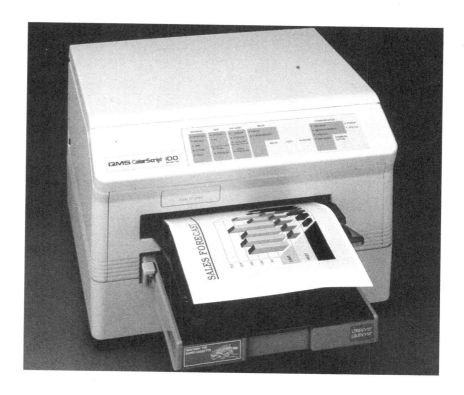

camera. Most cartridges come in one of two varieties: three-color and four-color. The three-color cartridges use cyan, yellow, and magenta as their primary colors, while the four-color versions add black. Cyan, yellow, and magenta can be combined to create black, but the printers generally get better results using all four primary colors, especially when producing text output in black ink. They require thermal paper or transparency film for best printing results.

Some of the leading manufacturers of 300-dpi thermal-transfer printers include QMS, Seiko, Oce Graphics, CalComp, and Tektronix. Mitsubishi and Sharp manufacture color printing engines used by some of these manufacturers.

Inkjet Printers

In an inkjet printer, ink in three or four of the primary color is sprayed through tiny nozzles on to the page. One recent trend in this category, pioneered by Tektronix and Dataproducts, is solid ink technology. The major advantage of solid-ink technology is that it can print on nearly any kind of paper stock. This is especially important when the printer is used as a proofing device, because the user can print on paper that more closely approximates the stock used to reproduce the output.

Solid ink is installed in the form of "color sticks" for each of the four primary colors: cyan, yellow, magenta, and black. The

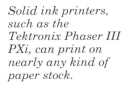

Solid ink printers, such as the Tektronix Phaser III PXi, can print on nearly any kind of paper stock.

ink melts almost instantly at a certain temperature, but solidifies just as quickly slightly below that temperature. When sprayed on the page, the ink dries before it can be absorbed, most of it remaining on the surface of the paper.

One limitation of solid-ink technology is that it does not do a good job of printing on transparencies. Solid inks tend to have a "beaded" texture that distorts light passing through the medium. Tektronix has addressed this problem with a proprietary fusing process that applies 3000 pounds of pressure to the printed surface. The result, Tektronix claims, is "projectable transparencies." However, thermal-transfer printers still do a better job of producing output on transparent media.

Iris Graphics offers a series of inkjet printers that can produce continuous-tone images on nearly any kind of paper stock. They are aimed largely at service bureaus and newspapers. But with price tags of $34,000 and higher, they are out of reach of most desktop publishing end-users.

Dye Sublimation Printers

Dye sublimation is a variation on thermal-transfer technology. A thermal print head transfers dye from a ribbon to the paper or film on which the image is to be printed. Unlike conventional thermal-transfer printers, which melt tiny dots of wax or plastic onto the page, dye-sublimation printers can vary the intensity of each dot. This makes it possible to produce continuous-tone images. However, the technology is limited to printing on transparency film or a special kind of thermal paper. These printers also tend to be quite expensive, with typical price tags of $20,000 or more. However, prices for dye sublimation printers have come down in recent years.

High-Resolution Imagesetters

Imagesetters capable of producing high-resolution monochrome and color separation output are descended from the phototypesetters first developed in the 1950s. Like these early ancestors, imagesetters produce output on photographic film or resin-coated paper. However, they are capable of producing complete page layouts, including images, unlike traditional phototypesetters that could only produce type galleys.

The history of the PostScript imagesetter begins in 1986, with Linotype's introduction of the Linotronic 100 and 300 along with the RIP 1. Three years earlier, Linotype had signed an agreement with Adobe Systems giving the PostScript devel-

The Linotronic 300 was one of the first imagesetters capable of producing PostScript output.

oper rights to use typefaces from the German manufacturer's extensive type library. As part of the deal, Linotype won the right to incorporate the PostScript language into its laser-driven phototypesetters.

These products were relatively primitive by current standards, but the basic technology remains the same. A PostScript file is produced with a desktop publishing or graphics package and downloaded from a personal computer to the raster image processor (RIP). Here, the PostScript language commands are converted into an electronic array of tiny dots. This information is passed to the image recorder, where a laser beam exposes the dots onto photosensitive film or paper. The photosensitive medium is then removed from the recorder and sent through a chemical processor, which produces the final output in much the same way a photo processing lab develops your snapshots.

The major limitation in these early imagesetters was the RIP. With its limited memory and speed, Linotype's original RIP 1 had difficulty handling complex pages, especially those that included halftones or other images. Subsequent RIPs have steadily improved in performance and imaging capabilities. Today's imagesetters are capable of producing color separations at 3000 dots per inch or more in addition to standard monochrome output.

The leading manufacturers of PostScript imagesetters include Linotype-Hell, Agfa Corp., Optronics, Varityper, and Birmy Graphics. Other imagesetter manufacturers are Bidco (which supplies imagesetters to Alphatype), ECRM (which supplies PelBox imaging engines to Autologic, Chelgraph, Hyphen, Monotype, and Varityper), Mannesman Scangraphic, Monotype, and Purup. However, Linotype-Hell retains the lion's share of the market, followed by Agfa.

At first, many publishing users saw PostScript imagesetters largely as a high-resolution alternative to the laser printer. They wanted crisp, highly readable text and line art, but shied away from producing halftones. Part of this was due to the short-sightedness of many service bureau managers, whose equipment and/or expertise were not up to producing gray-scale images. They would advise their clients to produce halftones by traditional photographic methods, arguing that this was cheaper and offered better quality than digital halftones produced on an imagesetter. This might have been true a few years ago, but not any more. With the availability of low-cost gray-scale scanners and image-editing software—along with advances in the imagesetters themselves—users can now produce high-quality digital halftones in a cost-effective manner.

Color Separations

The latest frontier in desktop imaging is color. The imagesetter, with its high resolution and ability to produce output on film, is a key component in most desktop color publishing strategies. But older imagesetters—some of which are still used in some service bureaus—have significant limitations in their color separation capabilities. One obvious limitation is the RIP. Older RIPs are adequate for producing gray-scale halftones, but often choke on memory-intensive color images. Newer RIPs include faster processors, extra memory, high-speed network interfaces, and other features to speed the production of color images. Some also include proprietary screening technologies to improve the appearance of color halftones.

Another major limitation is dot repeatability. To produce process color on a printing press, the user must provide separations corresponding to the four primary colors, cyan, yellow, magenta, and black (CYMK). When these primaries are combined in various percentages, they can produce a wide variety of acceptable colors. On the press each full-color image receives four impressions of ink—once for each separation. For this to work, however, each dot on each of the four separations must be positioned with a high degree of precision. Otherwise, the output will suffer from misregistration and moire patterns.

Early imagesetters designed primarily for monochrome output often were not up to this task. Though they were adequate for simple spot color jobs, they did not offer the kind of precise dot repeatability needed for quality process color work. The major culprit in this was the feeding mechanism used to pull the paper or film media through the image recorder. Most early imagesetters use a roller feed mechanism that, while adequate for monochrome output, cannot provide a precise alignment of dots from one separation to another.

Drum Recorders

Some manufacturers have responded to these limitations by improving the roll-feed (also known as capstan) mechanisms in their imagesetters. Others have introduced imagesetters that use a drum-based mechanism similar to what might be found in a high-end color prepress system. One pioneer in this area was Optronics, whose Colorsetter uses a rotating drum with registration pins—similar to the tractor feed sprockets on a dot matrix printer—along with a vacuum mechanism to hold the film in place. Optronics claims that this drum mechanism offers overall repeatability of 5 microns—about one-fifteenth the

Some imagesetters, such as the Optronics Colorsetter, use a drum-based mechanism similar to what might be found in a high-end color prepress system.

diameter of a human hair. The imagesetter also uses a proprietary halftone screening method to improve output quality. Other manufacturers of drum-based imagesetters include Scitex, Linotype-Hell, and Agfa Corp. In addition to offering a more precise feeding mechanism, some of these imagesetters provide a relatively large imaging area that allows production of signatures for use on a web press.

In addition to providing these high-end imagesetters for production of color separations, several manufacturers offer less expensive models for relatively modest imaging needs. These imagesetters, priced between $20,000 and $40,000, are primarily targeted at in-house publishing departments.

Though there are tremendous distinctions among low-end imagesetters, there are some features that most have in common. Most low-end devices include built-in RIPs, as opposed to the standalone processors sold with the pricier models. Some even use a software-based RIP, relying on the host computer to image the page before it is sent to the image recorder. These less-costly imagesetters also offer lower resolution than their costlier siblings. Nevertheless, most of these models can do a good job of producing gray-scale images along with high-quality text and line art. Some of the low-end imagesetters can also do a reasonable job of producing color separations, especially for newspapers and other publications with relatively modest quality requirements.

Prepress Links

Leading developers of high-end color prepress systems, including Crosfield, Scitex, Linotype-Hell, and Screen, have introduced products that provide links to PostScript-based desktop publishing systems. These links tend to be quite expensive, but they also offer the best of two worlds: the high-quality image output of a proprietary prepress system along with the convenience and control of desktop publishing. These links are most often found in traditional color separation houses, which can take advantage of the desktop publishing revolution while justifying their large investment in high-end prepress systems that can cost as much as $1 million.

In a typical scenario, the user submits a desktop publishing file along with color transparencies. The system operator scans the transparencies with a drum scanner and incorporates the images into the page layout. The operator then produces the color separations with images and text in place.

Digital Typefaces

No discussion of output devices would be complete without a discussion of type. Desktop publishing systems have come a long way in their ability to produce images, but production of readable type remains their most important function.

Desktop publishers hear the terms "font" and "typeface" used interchangeably, but it was not always so. In the pre-PostScript typesetting era, the term "typeface" referred to a specific design of type, such as Times Roman or Helvetica Bold. "Typeface family" referred to a group of typefaces installed as a unit, such as "Times Roman, Times Bold, Times Italic, and Times Bold Italic." "Font" referred to a specific typeface in a specific size, such as "14-point Times Bold."

These distinctions made sense at the time. In older typesetting systems, fonts were loaded in distinct sizes and styles. A typesetter equipped with 14-, 18-, 24-, and 36-point Times Bold, for example, would be unable to produce a headline in 30-point Times bold unless the operator added that font.

In contrast, most desktop publishing systems use "scalable fonts." Instead of loading fonts in distinct sizes, you load one copy of each typeface, such as Times and Helvetica in normal, bold, italic, and bold-italic styles. When the user specifies a type size in a desktop publishing program and prints the document, the PostScript software enlarges the typeface to the desired size.

Terminology

This is why the meaning of "font" has changed. To a PostScript user who can scale type to almost any size, "font" generally refers to a typeface or even an entire typeface family. "Typeface" generally refers to the design of the type. You don't hear people say, "I just installed 14- and 18-point Broadway." Instead, they've installed a copy of the Broadway display face that can be enlarged from four to 1000 points and any size in between (depending on the capabilities of your software).

In addition to changing terminology, the growth of desktop publishing has created a revolution in the way typefaces are sold. In the pre-desktop publishing era, typefaces were an integral part of the typesetting systems on which they were used. But with the sudden popularity of laser printers and other output devices, fonts became commodities in their own right.

Many long-established leaders in the typography business have taken advantage of this new demand for type, including Linotype-Hell, Agfa, URW, and Monotype. Linotype-Hell began offering PostScript fonts in August 1987 and its contributions represent about 50 percent of the current market. It offers the fonts under its own label and also through a licensing agreement with PostScript developer Adobe Systems. Adobe has also converted public domain typefaces and licensed designs from other sources such as ITC, and is also one of the leading typeface vendors in the microcomputer market.

In addition to the well-established typesetter manufacturers, many smaller companies have also entered the digital font market. Some limit themselves to producing a small number of original font designs. Others combine original typefaces with alternative versions of popular fonts like Times Roman and Helvetica. One of the best known companies in this category is Bitstream, which was founded in Cambridge, MA., by a number of former Linotype employees. Bitstream bills itself as the first independent "digital type foundry," capable of designing and selling typefaces for a wide variety of computer output devices, including PostScript printers and imagesetters. Bitstream's best-known typefaces are "Dutch" and "Swiss," which are renamed and redesigned versions of Linotype's Times Roman and Helvetica. Its large library also includes original type designs and typefaces licensed from independent type sources like ITC.

The original LaserWriter was sold with 13 resident fonts that have come to be known as the "LaserWriter 13." These include Linotype-Hell's Times Roman and Helvetica in normal, bold, italic, and bold italic styles, plus Courier, a public domain typeface once used in many typewriters, in the same four styles. The last of the "LaserWriter 13" is the Symbol font, which includes non-English characters used for special purposes like mathematical formulas. The LaserWriter Plus, an upgraded version of the LaserWriter, included 35 resident fonts that are known as the "LaserWriter 35." In addition to the fonts described above, they include Palatino, Avant-Garde, Bookman, New Century Schoolbook, and Helvetica Narrow in roman, bold, italic, and bold italic styles, plus two "specialty" fonts, Zapf Chancery and Zapf Dingbats. Zapf Chancery is an ornate, script-like typeface that would be well at home on a wedding invitation. Zapf Dingbats is a collection of symbols, such as snowflakes, check marks, and boxes, that help add spice to a document.

These fonts are said to be "resident" in the printer. A resident font is sold with the printer or imagesetter and resides there permanently. Users can produce any document that includes that typeface without "downloading" the font (copying it to the printer) beforehand. If a particular font is not resident, the user must download it to the laser printer or imagesetter. In most cases, the publishing software handles this automatically, but in other cases, the user must do this by means of a font downloading program.

Almost all PostScript printers sold these days include the "LaserWriter 13," and most include the additional 22 fonts in the LaserWriter Plus. The one exception is Helvetica Narrow, a "slimmed down" version of standard Helvetica. Though offered in many PostScript laser printers, most imagesetters use a similar typeface called Condensed Helvetica that offers better-looking results at high resolution.

Font Formats

The fonts sold by Adobe Systems and many other type vendors conform to a format known as "Type 1." However, some vendors offer other formats. Bitstream, for example, uses a format called Speedo, though it also offers Type 1 fonts. Agfa offers a font format called Intellifont, and URW provides the Nimbus Q format. One of the newest type formats is Apple's TrueType. The font format can be an important consideration if you plan to use certain kinds of software packages designed to manipulate font outlines. It is also important when considering various products that produce scalable type on the computer display.

These "screen fonts," as they are called, allow users to see a reasonably accurate representation of their typefaces displayed

Scalable screen font products like Adobe Type Manager offer a method for getting good-looking type on the screen. The type on the bottom, generated without ATM, suffers from the "jaggies," while the type on the top was generated with ATM.

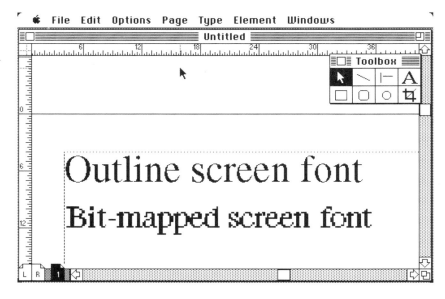

on your monitor. At first, all screen fonts, even those for PostScript devices, were bit maps. Users had to install the fonts in all the sizes and styles most commonly used. If a user specified a font of a different size, the display software enlarged the closest screen font as best it can. The problem was that the bit-mapped screen fonts took on a jagged appearance when enlarged or reduced. They looked fine when the page was printed, but they were difficult to read on the screen.

All this changed with the advent of scalable screen font programs like Adobe Type Manager (ATM) and Bitstream FaceLift. When you specify an odd point size on a system with ATM installed, the software creates a scaled rendition of the font without the jagged appearance. It does this in much the same way that PostScript creates type on a printer. The user must still install at least one bit-mapped version of the font along with the Adobe software, but there is no need to load multiple point sizes. Apple's TrueType, which is included in the Macintosh system and Microsoft Windows, provides built-in scalable screen fonts for those systems. However, the user must still install Adobe Type Manager or Bitstream FaceLift if they plan to use printer fonts from those vendors.

Chapter Ten

New Printing Technologies

Desktop publishing systems have radically altered the way that camera-ready layouts are produced. But once a page rolls off the laser printer or imagesetter, it is usually reproduced using the same methods printers have employed for many decades. Now, with the emergence of digital copiers and direct-to-plate imaging, electronic publishing technology is fast moving into the domain of the printing press.

There may soon be a time when "camera-ready artwork" is a thing of the past, relegated to the same museums that house hot-lead type and wooden presses. Instead of submitting pages to a print shop, customers will hand over a diskette containing a desktop-published document. That document will be reproduced in color or monochrome without most of the intermediate steps that now characterize the printing process: shooting a negative, stripping the film, making the plate, and so on.

This is not a far-future fantasy. Xerox, Kodak, Canon, and others have introduced digital photocopiers that can produce output directly from a desktop publishing system. Several companies offer products that allow direct production of printing plates from a PostScript imagesetter. One manufacturer even offers a color printing press with a digital link to desktop publishing systems.

In this chapter, we'll look at some of the ways that desktop publishing systems are having an impact on the reproduction of printed pages.

Direct-to-Film Output

Almost any PostScript imagesetter can easily produce output that skips the first step of the offset reproduction process: converting camera-ready pages into a film negative. In addition to producing output on resin-coated photographic paper, these imagesetters can produce output as film positives or negatives. To produce a film negative, for example, the user simply specifies that option when producing a PostScript file from the Print dialog box of the desktop publishing application. Some imagesetters can be set up to produce negative versions of the output file, in which case the user specifies film positive (the output is converted into a negative by the imagesetter).

Most PostScript service bureaus charge slightly more for film output than paper output, but film is often worth the extra expense. First, users can reduce their printing bills by removing the first step in the offset lithographic process. Second, they generally get better print quality because there is one less generation of the page. This is especially important when producing halftone images, because film generally does a better job of reproducing fine line screens. The only real advantage of paper is that it is easier to proofread.

Unfortunately, some managers in the printing industry refuse to accept film negatives. Many have spent large sums of money on camera equipment and feel that they need to recoup this investment by charging for production of film negatives. However, there are enough printers willing to accept film output that publishing users can simply take their jobs to a competitor. Instead of getting a little extra for a print job, the printer loses the business outright.

In addition to the ability to produce film negatives, most desktop publishing programs include a printing option that automatically adds crop and registration marks to the output. Many desktop publishing programs also offer a bleed option, allowing production of pages where an image extends to the edge of the page.

Electronic Stripping

Manual stripping, even for reproduction on a sheetfed press, represents one of the most time-consuming stages in the offset lithographic process. However, several software developers offer products that can automate the creation of impositions.

To get an idea of how impositions are created, try folding a sheet of letter-sized paper in half. Imagine it to be a four-page newspaper. Take a pen and label the pages: page 1 on the front, pages 2 and 3 on the inside, and page 4 on the back. Now unfold the sheet. On one side, you'll see pages 2 and 3 as you did before. But on the reverse side, pages 4 and 1 are next to each other, page 4 on the left and page 1 on the right.

Impositions produced on a large sheetfed or web press can include up to 64 pages. Some common imposition arrangements are shown here.

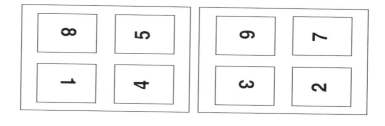

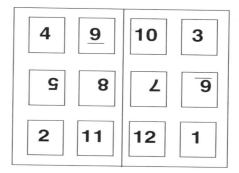

What you have created is a four-page signature for a newsletter or newspaper. The reader (hopefully) begins with page 1 and continues through page 4. But to the press operator, page 4 comes first, followed by 1, 2, and 3. By adding more signatures, you can increase the number of pages as much as you want—in multiples of four. Many newsletters are created in this manner, except they are printed on tabloid-sized paper instead of letter size. The tabloid size corresponds to two letter-sized sheets, so each of the four pages in the signature measures a full 8½×11 inches.

Because it fits within the 11×17-inch page size, this four-page imposition can be printed on a sheetfed press. But on a large sheetfed or web press, impositions can include between four and 64 pages. After the impositions are printed, they are folded and cut into signatures, which are then bound with other signatures into the book or magazine. The diagram above shows some of the ways pages can be arranged in these larger impositions. But the general idea remains the same: fold a sheet of paper into the desired number of pages, then label them in sequence. When you unfold the sheet, the labels will show you the correct positioning of the pages.

With a maximum page width of 18 inches or less, most imagesetters cannot create complete 16-page signatures (though imagesetters with larger imaging areas are becoming increasingly common). But users can create smaller, self-contained impositions, or create sections of larger ones. The four-page signature described above is relatively easy to create; users can also produce eight-page signatures in which each page is half-sized: $5^{1/2} \times 8^{1/2}$ inches. Even though these are true signatures, they can be produced on a sheetfed press, especially if the print shop has the necessary cutting, binding, and folding equipment.

The imagesetter can also produce sections of larger impositions. We have seen that an eight-page signature might have pages 6, 3, 4, and 5 on one side and pages 8, 1, 2, and 7 on the other. If you produce those two sets of pages separately on the imagesetter, the stripping job has been considerably simplified. Instead of stripping together eight pieces of film, the press operator need only deal with two.

When producing impositions on an imagesetter, be aware of the way pages are printed. Pages normally come out lengthwise, as they do in a laser printer. But to economize on space, you want the pages turned sideways. Some desktop publishing packages, such as Aldus PageMaker, provide this kind of control.

One problem in creating impositions is arranging pages in the correct sequence. Most desktop publishing programs were first designed when the laser printer was the only means of output. True to their origins, they still handle printing jobs as a series of pages in numerical sequence, starting with page 1. With many programs, users can rearrange pages and page numbers, but not without a great deal of difficulty.

This is where imposition software products come in. The first product in this category was Impostrip, from Ultimate Technographics in Montreal, Canada. Impostrip comes in several versions that work with specific desktop publishing packages, including Ventura Publisher, Aldus PageMaker, QuarkXPress, and the company's own publishing software. Its primary function is to convert PostScript files created by these programs into user-defined signatures. Users have a high degree of control over how signatures are produced. For example, you can account for the degree of page creep—the tendency of pages in the center of a saddle-stitched publication to extend beyond the bounds of the cover.

Other imposition programs include PressWise, from Aldus Corp., and InPosition, from DK&A of San Diego. PressWise works with a variety of desktop publishing programs, while InPosition works with QuarkXPress.

Mastering the art of imposition can save considerable amounts

*Software products
like Impostrip
offer an
automated
approach to
producing
impositions.*

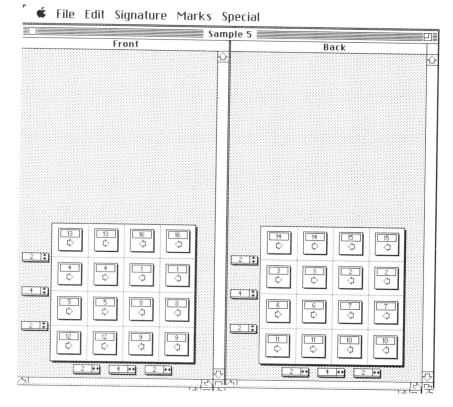

on printing costs while improving the appearance of your publication. Some commercial printers, for example, charge the same amount for producing a 12-page signature as they do for a 16-page signature. By effectively combining signatures, a customer can get more pages printed for the same amount of money.

Impositions are also important in color publishing. Whether you are producing spot or process color, it costs extra every time you run a set of sheets through a printing press. But if you print an extra color on one page, you can print it on all other pages on the same side of the signature for no extra cost. If you charge extra for color ads in your magazine or newspaper, your advertiser can underwrite the cost of printing editorial pages in color.

Direct-to-Plate

After pages have been stripped into place, the press operator creates one or more plates of metal or plastic. Here again, electronic publishing systems are providing a way to automate this process by offering direct-to-plate imaging technology.

Printware's 1440 Platesetter is a 1200-dpi PostScript-compatible output device that produces plates instead of pages.

Presstek has introduced a printing system that combines a Heidelberg sheetfed press with direct-to-plate imaging technology.

These products take several forms, including platemaking printers and imagesetting materials. One company, New Hampshire-based Presstek, has developed a complete color printing system that uses direct-to-plate technology.

Printware's 1440 Platesetter, one of the first direct-to-plate imaging products, is a 1200-dpi PostScript clone output device that produces paper or aluminum plates instead of pages. These plates, which conform to printing industry standards, can then be used on many sheetfed presses. Polychrome sells a version of the platemaking system under its own label.

Users of PostScript imagesetters can also produce plates directly from the desktop. 3M and Mitsubishi both sell plastic plates that can be used in most popular imagesetters, including the Linotronic 330 and Agfa 9800. Users can have their output produced on a plate without making any alterations to the original PostScript file. Of course, the customer (and press operator) needs to be sure that the plates are compatible with the press that will be used.

Going beyond the direct-to-plate product is the direct-to-press product. Presstek has introduced a printing system that combines a Heidelberg sheetfed press with direct-to-plate imaging technology. The system, which is capable of four-color process work, is used by Sir Speedy in its Digital QuickColor division to provide fast turnaround on color printing jobs. Though the quality of its color output is not outstanding, the technology holds great promise for the future.

Digital Photocopiers

High-speed xerographic printers and copiers represent one more potential alternative to lithography. Xerox Corp.'s Docutech system incorporates a 600-dpi scanner and 600-dpi laser printer, along with software that allows for pages and images to be stored and retrieved. Operating at 135 pages per minute, the system can automatically position, bind, and collate pages. It can also print a 100-line halftone with 256 levels of gray. Docutech is an expensive product, but it points the way toward future, scaled down copying systems that will offer similar capabilities.

Other manufacturers have also introduced digital copiers. Kodak's LionHeart, for example, is a 192-page-per-minute copier with a PostScript interface. Riso makes a duplicator that creates a 400-dpi stencil from a PostScript file and uses it to reproduce pages at 120 pages per minute.

Several color copiers also offer digital interfaces. Canon's Laser Copier offers a resolution of 400 dpi and the ability to image 256 gradations for each of the four primary colors (cyan, magenta, yellow, and black). Because it is a digital copier, it can produce such image effects as mosaics, textures, contours, and mirroring; electronic merging of elements; image repeat; and multi-page separation. Adobe Systems, working in cooperation with Canon, was the first company to offer a PostScript RIP for the copier. In 1991, Electronics for Imaging Inc., a new firm launched by Scitex founder Efi Arazi, introduced a controller

Xerox Corp.'s Docutech Production Publisher incorporates a 600-dpi scanner and 600-dpi laser printer, along with software that allows for pages and images to be stored and retrieved.

Digital interfaces for the Canon Color Laser Copier allow the use of the copier as a scanner or printer.

called Fiery Color Laser. Of particular interest to the graphic arts community is a color calibration and color management system that helps users verify that the specified color values are reproduced as faithfully as possible.

Other vendors with interfaces to the copier are Custom

Applications Inc., with its Freedom of Press PostScript clone, and Colorbus. Instead of producing PostScript output, the Colorbus product relies on Adobe Type Manager plus QuickDraw on the Macintosh or Zenographics' Pixie on Windows machines. Photographic images are passed directly to the copier, thus using the copier's ability to produce continuous-tone images, rather than digital halftones. According to Colorbus, this not only produces superior quality to PostScript's halftoning, it also speeds up output dramatically.

Eastman Kodak and Xerox Corp. have also introduced digital color copiers. The Kodak ColorEdge 1550 copier uses a copying engine from Canon that is similar to the one used in the CLC. Kodak added some original pieces to the printer, including a 35-mm slide scanner and proprietary driver software for the Macintosh. Both CAI and Colorbus already have drivers for the ColorEdge copiers.

Unlike Kodak, Xerox developed its own product, the Xerox 5775 Digital Color Copier. It features 400-dpi resolution with a total palette of 64 colors. The print speed is higher than Canon's: 7.5 pages per minute for full-color letter pages. The product offers image-editing and image-manipulation functions accessed through a touch-screen CRT.

Products like these should provide a major boon for the printing industry, some of which has been slow to adjust to the desktop publishing revolution. With direct-to-plate imaging products and digital copiers, printing operations are likely to take on more of the functions currently associated with service bureaus. Printing companies will benefit by offering extra services to their customers, and customers will benefit by having a one-stop solution for their publishing needs.

Glossary

Algorithm. A set of rules for solution of problems, represented by a sequence of stored instructions. Computer programs are an example of algorithms.

AppleTalk. A local-area network protocol developed by Apple Computer for use with the Macintosh.

Architecture. The specific components, and the way those components are interconnected, that make up a microcomputer system. Often used to describe the specific bus structure within a microcomputer.

ASCII. American Standard Code for Information Interchange. A standard coding system that assigns a numeric value to letters, numbers, and symbols.

ASCII File. A text file containing ASCII characters only. The lowest common denominator for exchanging text among programs. Almost any word processor or desktop publishing program can read or write ASCII files. Also known as text-only files.

Aspect Ratio. The relationship between the height and width of a displayed object. A 1:1 aspect ratio means the object will appear undistorted.

Auto Trace. A feature found in some graphics programs that allows conversion of bit-mapped images into an object-oriented format. See Bit-map, Object-oriented graphics.

Bernoulli. A removable hard disk system popular in the PC-compatible. Bernoulli disks can hold 44 or 90 megabytes of data and are manufactured by Iomega Corp.

Bezier curves. A type of curve created by some object-oriented graphics programs that can be manipulated by means of end-points and anchor points that determine its slope and length.

Binary. A numbering system employed by most computer systems that uses two numerals, 0 and 1, to represent all numbers.

Bit. The smallest unit of binary information. A bit will have a value of "1" or "0." A contracted acronym derived from Binary digIT.

Bit-Map. Images formed by patterns of dots, as opposed to object-oriented images, where shapes are formed from mathematical descriptions.

Bit-Mapped Display. A computer display that can control individual pixels, allowing the computer to show graphics in addition to text. See Character-Based Display.

Block. A unit of text or graphics that can be manipulated as a whole.

Brightness. A measure of lightness or darkness in an image.

Bus. A data pathway within a computer system.

Byte. A unit of data containing eight bits. A byte can consist of up to 256 different values. Used as a measure of file size on a computer. See Kilobyte, Megabyte.

Calibration. A process by which a scanner, monitor, or output device is adjusted to provide more accurate display and reproduction of images.

Camera-Ready Copy. Text and illustrations laid out on a page in the proper size and position, and ready to be photographed by a graphic arts camera. See Mechanicals.

Cathode-Ray Tube (CRT). A vacuum tube that generates

and guides electrons onto a fluorescent screen to produce images, characters, or graphics.

CCD. See Charge-Coupled Device.

Central Processing Unit (CPU). The main section of a computer, which handles arithmetic and logic operations.

CGA. Short for Color Graphics Adapter, the first color display standard for PC-compatible computers. Offers limited resolution. See EGA, Hercules, VGA.

CGM. See Computer Graphics Metafile.

Character-Based Display. A computer display, commonly found in the first personal computers, that is limited to showing alphanumeric characters and simple graphic elements. Most character-based displays use a grid consisting of 25 rows and 80 columns. Each cell in the grid can contain only a single character.

Charge-Coupled Device (CCD). An image sensor used in scanners and digital cameras.

Clipboard. A temporary electronic storage area in a computer system where text or graphics can be held for reuse.

Color Correction. A process of adjusting color values to achieve the best level of accuracy for a reproduction.

Color Proof. A sample of a color page usually produced to verify that the colors will be printed correctly. Most color proofs are produced using film-based systems like Du Pont's Cromalin or 3M's Color Keys. However, the term is sometimes used to refer to color prints produced on 300-dpi thermal transfer printers.

Color Separation. A process by which a color page is converted into CYMK color components. Each color can be used to create a piece of film, which is burned onto a plate or written directly to a printing press. See CYMK.

Color Separations. A set of four transparencies for making plates in four-color printing.

Comp. See Comprehensive.

Comprehensive. A page, produced during the design process, that provides a preview of how the final print job will look.

Computer Graphics Metafile (CGM). A file format used for storing computer graphics.

Continuous Tone. A photograph or illustration containing an infinite range of colors or gray shades.

Contrast. A measure of the difference among various colors or gray levels in an image. A high-contrast image shows a large difference between light and dark shades. A low-contrast image shows less difference between light and dark shades.

CP/M. An early operating system for microcomputers developed by Digital Research Inc.

CPU. See Central Processing Unit.

Crop. To cut or trim an illustration or other graphic element.

Crop marks. Small marks on a page that indicate the area to be printed.

CRT. See Cathode-Ray Tube.

CYMK. Cyan, Yellow, Magenta, Black. These four colors are used by printers to reproduce color images.

Data Compression. An operation that reduces the memory space required to store image data.

Default. A specification that takes effect in the absence of other instructions. Most scanner programs have default settings for variables like brightness and contrast that apply unless the user requests something else.

Densitometer. A device used to measure the intensity of gray shades or colors in a printed image. Often used to calibrate an imagesetter, scanner, or monitor for more accurate display and reproduction of images.

Desktop Publishing. The use of a personal computer to produce camera-ready page layouts for books, newsletters, magazines, and other printed material. Also refers to programs that produce page layouts. See Page-Makeup Program.

Dialog Box. A pop-up window in a program that allows the user to choose among different options.

Diffusion. A filtering effect performed on gray-scale or color images that randomly distributes gray levels in small areas of an image to achieve a mezzotint effect.

Digital Halftone. A halftone produced by a computer system. See Halftone.

Digitize. To convert information to the digital format usable by a computer. What scanners and digitizers do.

Digitizer. A device that converts video signals into a digital format that can be displayed on a computer. Also used to refer to certain computer drawing devices.

Disk Operating System (DOS). An operating system for IBM-compatible personal computers that controls basic computer operations, such as the transfer of data to and from a disk drive. Requires use of English-like commands to perform operations. Also known as MS-DOS and PC-DOS.

Dithering. A process by which an input or output device simulates shades of gray in an image by grouping dots into clusters known as halftone cells. See Halftone Cell.

DOS. See Disk Operating System.

Dot. The smallest unit that can be printed, scanned, or displayed on a monitor. Dots produced on a laser printer are sometimes called spots.

Dots Per Inch (DPI). A unit that describes the resolution of an output device or monitor.

DPI. See Dots Per Inch.

Driver. A software program that controls a specific hardware device such as a frame grabber board, scanner, or printer.

Drum Imagesetter. An imagesetter in which the output media is mounted on a rotating drum.

Drum Scanner. A scanner in which reflective or transmissive media are mounted on a rotating drum.

Dye Sublimation. A color printing technology used in continuous-tone printers.

Edge Enhancement. An operation that accentuates the edge details of an image.

EGA. Short for Enhanced Graphics Adapter, a color display standard in the PC-compatible environment. Offers better resolution and color display than CGA, but is surpassed by VGA. See CGA, Hercules, VGA.

Encapsulated PostScript (EPS). A file format that stores images in the form of PostScript language commands.

EPS. See Encapsulated PostScript.

Equalization. A process by which the range of gray or color shades in an image is expanded to make the image more attractive.

Facsimile. A technology that allows transmission of images over telephone lines by use of facsimile machines or PC fax boards.

Filter. A software function that modifies an image by altering the gray or color values of certain pixels.

FinePrint. A printing technology developed by Apple Computer that improves the resolution of text produced on a laser printer. See PhotoGrade, Resolution Enhancement Technology, TurboRes.

Flatbed Scanner. A type of scanner, resembling a small photocopier, in which the image to be scanned is placed on a glass platen.

Font. All letters, numbers, and symbols in one size and type-face. Helvetica Bold Italic is a typeface. 12-point Helvetica bold italic is a font. "Font" is sometimes used interchangeably with "Typeface."

Four-Color Printing. A process that allows a printing press to reproduce most colors by mixing the three primary colors (cyan, yellow, magenta) and black.

Frame. A block positioned on a page into which the user can place text or graphics.

Frame Buffer. Memory used to store an array of graphic or pictorial image data. Each element of the array corresponds to one or more pixels in a video display or one or more dots on a laser printer or other output device.

Frame-Grabber Board. An image processing board that samples, digitizes, stores, and processes video signals. Typically, a frame grabber board will plug into one expansion slot within a microcomputer.

Galley. In typesetting terminology, a reproduction of a column of type, usually printed on a long paper sheet.

Gamma Correction. A process by which the user adjusts the midtone contrast and brightness of an image.

Gamma Curve Editor. A function found in many imaging programs that allows the user to perform gamma correction operations on a color or gray-scale image. Also known as a Gray Map Editor.

GEM. Short for Graphics Environment Manager, a graphical operating environment used by many publishing and graphics programs. Developed by Digital Research, Inc.

Graphical User Interface (GUI). A computer interface, such as the Macintosh system or Microsoft Windows, characterized by the use of a bit-mapped display and graphical icons that represent common computer functions.

Gray Scale. A measure of the number of gray levels in an image. Also used to describe the ability to display multiple levels of gray.

Gray Scale Value. A number with a range between 0 and 256 that represents the brightness level of an individual pixel in a gray scale image document.

GUI. See Graphical User Interface.

Halftone. A type of photograph that can be reproduced by a printing press. A halftone breaks a continuous-tone photo into tiny dots, which the press can reconstruct with ink. The eye interprets the dots as tones and shades. The density of the dot pattern, called a screen, determines the ultimate quality of the printed reproduction. A halftone can be a positive or a negative. See Screen.

Halftone Cell. A halftone dot created on a laser printer or imagesetter. The cell is created by grouping printer dots into a grid. The more dots present in the grid, the larger the cell appears.

Hand Scanner. A small scanner that requires the user to manually move the unit over the image to be scanned.

Hardware. Mechanical, magnetic, electronic, and electrical devices that make up a computer. Physical equipment that makes up a computer system.

Hercules. A monochrome graphics display standard used in the PC-compatible environment. See CGA, EGA, VGA.

Histogram. A graph showing the distribution of gray or color levels within an image. The horizontal coordinate is the pixel value. The vertical coordinate shows the number of pixels in the image that use the value. Histograms give a good indication of image contrast and brightness dynamic range.

Horizontal Resolution. The number of pixels contained in a single horizontal scanning line.

Illustration Program. A program used to create object-oriented graphics. See Object-Oriented Graphics.

Imagesetter. A high-resolution output device, descended from the phototypesetter, that produces output on film or photographic paper at resolutions of 1000 dots per inch or more. Usually employs a page description language like PostScript.

Inkjet Printer. A nonimpact printer that uses droplets of ink. As a printhead moves across surface of paper, it shoots stream of tiny, electrostatically-charged ink drops at page, placing them to form characters.

Interpolation. A mathematical technique used in some scanning and graphics programs that can be used to increase the apparent resolution of an image. Computers usually store images as numbers that represent the intensity of the image at discrete points. Interpolation generates values for points in between these discrete points by looking at the surrounding intensities.

Joint Photographic Experts Group (JPEG). An international standard for compression and decompression of photographic images.

JPEG. See Joint Photographic Experts Group.

Kerning. The reduction of space between characters to make them fit more tightly.

Kilobyte. A measurement unit used to describe the size of computer files. A kilobyte is equivalent to 1024 bytes or characters of information.

Landscape. Horizontal orientation of pages or screen displays. See Portrait.

Laser Printer. A non-impact output device that fuses toner to paper to create near-typeset quality text and graphics. The basic technology is similar to that of a photocopier.

Layout. The arrangement of a page, especially the spacing and position of text and graphics. Often used to describe a rough sketch.

LCD. See Liquid-Crystal Display.

LED. See Light-Emitting Diode.

Ligatures. Two or more letters that touch to form a single unit when placed next to each other.

Light-Emitting Diode (LED). A form of display lighting employed on many different office, reprographic, and consumer products.

Line Art. A drawing that contains no grays or middle tones. Even when cross-hatching and other techniques are used to simulate shading, line art is made up exclusively of black (lines) and white (paper). In Ventura Publisher, line art refers to object-oriented graphics.

Line Screen. A measure of the screen frequency, or resolution, of a halftone. Most printed halftones have line screens ranging from 65 lines per inch to 150 lines per inch.

Linotronic. The brand name for imagesetters manufactured by Linotype-Hell, including the Linotronic 330 and Linotronic 630.

Liquid-Crystal Display (LCD). LCD screens are made up of liquid crystals sandwiched between two glass plates. They are typically small and flat, and require very little power for operation.

Lithography. See Offset Printing.

Local-Area Network. A system that connects microcomputers to one another, allowing them to share data and output devices.

Lossless. An image-compression function in which image data is not lost every time the compression is performed.

Lossy. An image-compression function in which image data is lost every time the compression is performed.

LPI. Abbreviation for lines per inch. Used to measure halftone resolution.

MacPaint. A paint program developed for the Macintosh

computer and sold by Claris Corp. Also refers to the 72-dpi image format supported by MacPaint and many other programs.

Mail-Merge. A function, found in most word processing programs, that allows the user to create personalized form letters.

Mechanicals. Camera-ready pages on artboards or flats, with text and art in position. See Camera-Ready Copy.

Megabyte. A measurement unit used to describe the size of computer files. A megabyte is equivalent to 1024 kilobytes, or 1,048,576 characters of information.

Microprocessor. A single chip or integrated circuit containing an entire central processing unit for a personal computer or computer-based device.

Microsoft Windows. A software application developed by Microsoft that manages data displayed on the CRT screen in rectangular areas known as windows. The user interacts with the software by selecting icons and menu items from the screen.

Modem. A device that allows computers to send and receive information over phone lines.

Moire Pattern. An undesirable pattern in a digital halftone resulting from the superimposition of dot-screens at wrong screen angles. Usually occurs when a halftone has been rescanned or if a dithered image has been scaled.

Monospaced font. A type style with an equal amount of space allotted for each character. Most typewriters produce monospaced characters.

Mouse. A small, hand-held device for positioning the cursor on the screen. When the mouse is rolled across the surface of the desk, the cursor moves a corresponding distance on the screen.

MS-DOS. A disk operating system used widely with personal computers and developed by Microsoft Corp.

MSP. The graphics format used by Microsoft Windows Paint.

Multiple Masters. A font-rendering technology developed by Adobe Systems that can reproduce the characteristics of almost any typeface.

National Television Standards Committee. The committee that developed the analog video signal standard—NTSC—used by the broadcast television industry in North America.

NTSC. See National Television Standards Committee.

Object-Oriented Graphics. Graphic images created by means of mathematical descriptions. They can usually be displayed or printed at the full resolution of the monitor or output device, offering more precision than bit-mapped images.

OCR. See Optical Character Recognition.

Offset Printing. A widely used printing process in which a page is reproduced photographically on a metal plate that is then attached to a revolving cylinder. Ink is transferred from the plate to a rubber blanket from which it is transferred to paper.

Omnifont. A capability found in some OCR programs that allows them to recognize almost any font without pre-training.

Operating System. Master programs that keep all of computer components working together, including application programs.

Optical Character Recognition. The process by which text on paper is scanned and converted into text files in a computer.

Optical Disk. A form of data storage in which a laser records data on a disk that can be read with a lower-power laser pickup. There are three types of optical disks: Read Only (RO), Write-Once Read Many (WORM), and two types of erasable—Thermo Magneto Optical (TMO) and Phase Change (PC).

Orphan. A short line of text that appears at the top of a column. Many designers consider orphans to be undesirable, and some page-makeup programs can automatically remove them. See Widow.

OS/2. An operating system for microcomputers developed by Microsoft and IBM.

Overlay. A sheet laid on top of a page for spot-color printing.

Page Description Language. A programming language, such as PostScript, that gives precise instructions for how a page should look to an output device. See PostScript.

Page-Makeup Program. A computer program that allows the user to create page layouts for newsletters, newspapers, magazines, and other printed materials. Also known as desktop publishing or page layout programs.

Paint Program. A program used to create bit-mapped graphics. See Bit-Map.

Palette. The set of all colors available for screen displays.

Panning. Moving a graphic image inside a frame to see its various sections.

Pantone Matching System. A popular system for specifying spot colors. Each color has its own Pantone number by which it can be selected. See Spot Color.

PC-Compatible. A computer system compatible with the IBM-PC and its descendants.

PCX. A graphic file format produced by PC Paintbrush. Supported by many scanners and publishing programs.

PhotoGrade. A printing technology developed by Apple Computer that improves the quality of halftones produced on a laser printer. See FinePrint, Resolution Enhancement Technology, TurboRes.

Pica. A printing measurement unit used to specify line lengths, margins, columns, gutters, and so on. Equivalent to 12 points, or about 1/6 of an inch.

PICT. An image format used by many Macintosh graphics programs. Originally designed for object-oriented graphics, but can display bit-mapped images as well.

Pixel. A picture element, or the smallest addressable component of a displayable image. Used to describe resolution.

Plate. A thin, flexible sheet of metal, paper, or plastic used in offset printing. It contains a photographic reproduction of the page.

Point Size. The vertical measurement of type, equivalent to the distance between the highest ascender and lowest descender.

Point. A unit of measurement used in printing and typography that is roughly equivalent to 1/72 of an inch.

Portrait. Vertical orientation of a page or display. See Landscape.

Position Stat. A photocopy or other reproduction of a halftone that is pasted onto a mechanical to show the printer how to crop and position the final image.

Posterization. A photographic effect in which the number of gray levels in an image is reduced to achieve a poster-like effect.

PostScript. A page description language developed by Adobe Systems Inc. and used by many laser printers and imagesetters. See Page description language.

PostScript Clone. A page description language that emulates PostScript. In theory, a PostScript clone printer can produce any page that a true PostScript printer can produce.

Print Spooler. A program that temporarily stores a file to be printed until the output device is available.

Process Camera. A camera used in graphic arts to photograph mechanicals and create printing plates.

Process Colors. The four colors needed for four-color printing: yellow, magenta, cyan, and black. See Four-Color Printing.

Proof. A trial copy of a page or publication used to check accuracy. Also short for proofread, meaning to check for mistakes.

Protocol. A formal set of conventions governing format of data and control of information exchange between two communication devices.

QuickDraw. The portion of the Apple Macintosh operating system that handles screen display and other graphics functions.

RAM. See Random Access Memory.

Random Access Memory (RAM). Computer memory that can be read and changed. Data can be written to a particular location without having to sequence through previous locations. RAM is volatile, so all data is lost on power down.

Raster Graphics. Pictures sent to printer as bit maps (each element of a picture is a dot defined as black or white).

Raster-Image Processor (RIP). A piece of hardware that electronically prepares a page created on a computer system for output on an imagesetter or other device.

Read Only Memory (ROM). Computer memory containing fixed data that cannot be changed once programmed. Programming is accomplished during the manufacturing process.

Reflective Media. Print media, such as paper, that show images by reflecting light back to the eye.

Register. Precise alignment of printed images, printing plates, or negatives.

Registration Marks. Marks used to permit exact alignment of pages. Usually printed just outside the live area and then trimmed off. The standard register mark is a small circle with a cross inside.

Resolution. The density of dots or pixels on a page or display, usually measured in dots per inch. The higher the resolution, the smoother the appearance of text or graphics.

Resolution Enhancement Technology. A printing technology developed by Hewlett-Packard that improves the resolution of text produced on a laser printer. See FinePrint, PhotoGrade, TurboRes.

RGB. An abbreviation for Red, Green, and Blue, the primary colors used in CRT display devices.

ROM. See Read Only Memory.

Sans Serif. Typestyles without little strokes known as serifs, such as Helvetica and Avant Garde. Sometimes called block or gothic.

Scalable Fonts. Fonts that can be scaled to any size from a single set of masters without loss of quality.

Scale. To change the size of a piece of artwork.

Scanner. A digitizing device that converts a piece of artwork into an electronic bit-map that can be loaded and manipulated by a software program. A means of converting hand-drawn art or photos into electronic form.

Screen. The pattern of dots used to make a halftone or tint. Halftone screens are measured in lines, equivalent to dots per inch. Tint screens are measured in percentages, with a 10-percent screen being very light and a 100-percent screen being totally black.

Screen Fonts. Digital typefaces used for screen display.

SCSI. See Small Computer Systems Interface.

Search-and-Replace. A function, found in word processors and desktop publishing programs, that allows the user to search for a certain string of characters and replace it with a another string of characters.

Separations. Transparencies or pages used for color reproduction. Each separation is used to reproduce a particular color. See Process Color, Four-Color Printing.

Serif. A tiny decorative stroke in character designs. Serif typefaces, such as Times or Palatino, use serifs in their designs. See Sans Serif.

Sharpen. A filtering effect that enhances contrast around edges in an image.

Slide Scanner. An image scanner capable of scanning 35-mm slides.

Small Computer Systems Interface (SCSI). An interface for connecting disks and other peripheral devices to computer systems. SCSI is defined by an American National Standards Institute (ANSI) standard and is widely used throughout the computer industry.

Soften. A filtering effect that decreases contrast in an image.

Solarization. A photographic effect achieved when a negative is briefly exposed to light. Some areas of the image are under-exposed, while others are overexposed.

Spell-Check. A function found in word processors and desktop publishing programs that identifies and corrects misspelled words.

Spot Color. The use of one or more extra colors on a page, used to highlight specified page elements. Colors are usually speci-fied as PMS codes. See Pantone Matching System.

Stripping. The act of combining and positioning film negatives or positives together as a single unit, or film flat, that is used to image the printing plate.

SyQuest. A removable hard disk system popular on the Macintosh. SyQuest disks can hold 44 or 90 megabytes of data and are manufactured by several vendors.

Tagged Image File Format (TIFF). A graphics file format used to store color and gray-scale images.

Thermal Transfer. A technology used in many color printers in which ink or dye is transferred to the page using a heat process.

386. A computer system that uses the 80386 microprocessor from Intel.

Thumbnail. A rough layout of a page, usually used for planning purposes.

TIFF. See Tagged Image File Format.

Transmissive Media. Film-based media, such as 35-mm slides or transparencies, that require backlighting to be seen.

TrueType. A typeface format developed by Apple Computer.

TurboRes. A printing technology developed by LaserMaster Corp. that improves the resolution of text produced on a laser printer. See FinePrint, PhotoGrade, Resolution Enhancement Technology.

Type 1. A format for storing digital typefaces developed by Adobe Systems. The most popular typeface format for PostScript printers.

Typeface. A particular type design. See Font, Typeface Family.

Typeface Family. A set of all the different variations—wide, narrow, italic, bold, bold italic—of a given type design. Helvetica is a type family. See Font.

UCR. See Undercolor Removal.

Undercolor Removal (UCR). A process that increased the quality of color reproduction by changing the balance of inking. The amount of ink used to print yellow, magenta, and cyan in dark areas is decreased, while black is increased to produce a stronger image.

UNIX. A general-purpose, multiuser, interactive operating system originally developed by AT&T Bell Laboratories.

Unsharp Masking Enhancement. An operation that produces a sharpened version of an image.

VGA. Short for Video Graphics Array, a popular color display standard in the PC-compatible environment. See CGA, EGA, Hercules.

Virtual Memory. A hardware and software mechanism in which a hard disk is used as an extension of RAM.

Widow. A short line of text that appears at the bottom of a paragraph or column. Many designers consider widows to be undesirable, and some page-makeup programs can automatically remove them. See Orphan.

Word Processor. A program used to enter, edit, and manipulate text.

Workstation. A full-featured desktop or deskside computer typically dedicated to a single person's use.

WYSIWYG. An acronym for What You See Is What You Get, meaning that text and graphics on a screen correspond closely to final printed output. Pronounced wizzy-wig.

Zoom. To view an enlarged (zoom in) or reduced (zoom out) portion of a page on screen.

Vendor Listings

Graphics Software

Adobe Illustrator
Adobe Systems Inc.
1585 Charleston Rd.
Mountain View, CA 94039
(415) 961-4400

Aldus Freehand
Aldus Corp.
411 First St. South, Suite 200
Seattle, WA 98104
(206) 622-5500

Arts and Letters
Computer Support Corp.
15926 Midway Rd.
Dallas, TX 74244
(214) 661-8960

Canvas
Deneba Software
3305 N.W. 74th Ave.
Miami, FL 33122
(305) 594-6965

ColorStudio
Fractal Design
101 Madeline Dr. Suite 204
Aptos, CA 95003
(408) 688-8800

Corel Draw
Corel Systems Corp.
Corel Building, 1600 Carling
Ottawa, Canada, K1Z 7M4
(613) 728-8200

DeskPaint/DeskDraw
Zedcor
4500 E. Speedway #22
Tucson, AZ 85712
(602) 881-8101

Digital Darkroom
Aldus Corp.
411 First St. South, Suite 200
Seattle, WA 98104
(206) 622-5500

GEM Artline
Digital Research Inc.
60 Garden Court
Monterey, CA 93942
(408) 646-6208

Gray FX
Xerox Imaging Systems
185 Albany St.
Cambridge, MA 02139
(617) 864-4700

Harvard Draw
Software Publishing Corp.
3165 Kifer Road
Santa Clara, CA 95051
(408) 986-8000

HotShot Graphics
SymSoft Corp.
Call Box 5
924 Incline Way
Incline Village, NV 89540
(702) 832-4300

Image-In Color/Color Professional
Image-In Inc.
406 E. 79th St.
Minneapolis, MN 55420
(612) 888-3633

ImageStudio
Fractal Design
101 Madeline Drive Suite 204
Aptos, CA 95003
(408) 688-8800

MacDraw/MacPaint
Claris Corp.
5201 Patrick Henry Dr.
Santa Clara, CA 95052
(408) 987-7000

Micrografx Designer
Micrografx Inc.
1303 Arapaho
Richardson, TX 75081
(214) 234 1769

PC Paintbrush
ZSoft Corp.
450 Franklin Rd., #100
Marietta, GA 30067
(404) 428-0008

PhotoFinish
ZSoft Corp.
450 Franklin Rd., Suite 100
Marietta, GA 30067
(404) 428-0008

Photoshop
Adobe Systems
1585 Charleston Rd.
Mountain View, CA 94039
(415) 961-4400

PhotoStyler
Aldus Corp.
411 First St. South, Suite 200
Seattle, WA 98104
(206) 622-5500

Picture Publisher
Micrografx Inc.
1303 Arapaho
Richardson, TX 75081
(214) 234 1769

SmartArt
Adobe Systems
1585 Charleston Rd.
Mountain View, CA 94039
(415) 961-4400

Streamline
Adobe Systems
1585 Charleston Rd.
Mountain View, CA 94039
(415) 961-4400

SuperPaint
Aldus Corp.
411 First St. South, Suite 200
Seattle, WA 98104
(206) 622-5500

Fonts/Font Software

Adobe Type Library
Adobe Systems
1585 Charleston Rd.
Mountain View, CA 94039
(415) 961-4400

Adobe Type Manager
Adobe Systems
1585 Charleston Rd.
Mountain View, CA 94039
(415) 961-4400

Bitstream Type Library
Bitstream Inc.
Athenaeum House
215 1st St.
Cambridge, MA 02142
(617) 497-6222

FaceLift
Bitstream Inc.
Athenaeum House
215 1st St.
Cambridge, MA 02142
(617) 497-6222

Font Studio
Letraset U.S.A.
40 Eisenhower Drive
Paramus, NJ 07653
(201) 845-6100

Fontographer
Altsys Corp.
720 Ave, F, Suite 108
Plano, TX 75074
(214) 424-4888

Linotype Type Library
Linotype Co.
425 Oser Ave.
Hauppauge, NY 11788
(516) 434-2717

Master Juggler
Alsoft Corp.
P.O. Box 927
Spring, TX 77383
(713) 353-1510

Publisher's Type Foundry
ZSoft Corp.
450 Franklin Rd., Suite 100
Marietta, GA 30067
(404) 428-0008

Treacyfaces
Treacyfaces
111 Sibley Ave., 2nd floor
Ardmore, PA 19003
(215) 896-0860

TypeStyler
Broderbund Software Inc.
17 Paul Drive
San Rafael, CA 94903
(415) 492-3200

OCR Software

Accutext
Xerox Imaging Systems
185 Albany St.
Cambridge, MA 02139
(617) 864-4700

OmniPage
Caere Corp.
100 Cooper Ct.
Los Gatos, CA 95030
(408) 395-7000

ReadRight
OCR Systems
1800 Byberry Rd., Suite 1405
Huntington Valley, PA 19006
(215) 938-7460

Recognita
Recognita Corp. of America
1250 Oakmead Pkwy., Suite 210
Sunnyvale, CA 94088
(408) 749-9935

WordScan
Calera Recognition Systems
2500 Augustine Dr.
Santa Clara, CA 95054
(408) 986-8006

Page-Makeup Software

Aldus PageMaker
Aldus Corp.
411 First St. South, Suite 200
Seattle, WA 98104
(206) 622-5500

Archetype Designer
Archetype Inc.
100 Fifth Ave.
Waltham, MA 02154
(617) 890-7544

DesignStudio/Ready,Set,Go!
Manhattan Graphics
250 East Hartsdale Ave. #23
Hartsdale, NY 10530
(914) 725-4924

Finesse
Logitech Inc.
6505 Kaiser Dr.
Fremont, CA 94555
(415) 795-8500

FrameMaker
Frame Technology
1010 Rincon Circle
San Jose, CA 95131
(408) 433-1928

Interleaf Publisher
Interleaf Inc.
10 Canal Park
Cambridge, MA 02141
(617) 577-9800

Legacy
NBI Inc.
3450 Mitchell Ln.
Boulder, CO 80301
(303) 444-5710

Microsoft Publisher
Microsoft Corp.
10611 NE 36th St.
Redmond, WA 98073
(206) 882-8080

Publish-It
Timeworks Inc.
625 Academy Dr.
Northbrook, IL 60062
(708) 559-1300

QuarkXPress
Quark Inc.
300 S. Jackson St., Suite 100
Denver, CO 80209
(303) 934-2211

Ventura Publisher
Ventura Software Inc.
15175 Innovation Dr.
San Diego, CA 92128
(619) 673-7537

Printing Software

Freedom of Press
Custom Applications Inc.
900 Middlesex Turnpike
Billerica, MA 01821
(508) 667-8585

Impostrip
Ultimate Technographics Inc.
4980 Buchon St., Suite 403
Montreal, Canada, H4P 1S8
(514) 733-1188

In Position
DK&A
1010 Turquoise St. #301
San Diego, CA 92108
(619) 488-8118

Pre-Print
Aldus Corp.
411 First Street South, Suite 200
Seattle, WA 98104
(206) 622-5500

PressWise
Aldus Corp.
411 First Street South, Suite 200
Seattle, WA 98104
(206) 622-5500

SpectreSeps/SpectrePrint
Pre-Press Technologies Inc.
2443 Impala Dr.
Carlsbad, CA 92008
(619) 931-2695

Ventura Separator/Color Pro
Ventura Software, Inc.
15175 Innovation Drive
San Diego, CA 92128
(619) 673- 7525

Word Processing Software

Ami Professional
Lotus Development Corp.
55 Cambridge Pkwy.
Cambridge, MA 02142
(617) 577-8500

MacWrite II
Claris Corp.
5201 Patrick Henry Dr.
Santa Clara, CA 95052
(408) 987-7000

Microsoft Word
Microsoft Corp.
10611 NE 36th St.
Redmond, WA 98073
(206) 882-8080

Nisus
Paragon Concepts
990 Highland Dr., Suite 312
Solana Beach, CA 92075
(619) 481-1477

Signature
XyQuest
3 Loomis St.
Bedford, MA 01730
(617) 275-4439

WordPerfect
WordPerfect Corp.
1555 N. Technology Way
Orem, UT 84057
(800) 451-5151

WordStar
WordStar International
201 Alameda del Prado
Novato, CA 94949
(415) 382-8000

Write Now
T/Maker
2115 Landings Dr.
Mountain View, CA 94043
(415) 962-0195

Color Proofing Systems

Color Keys/MatchPrint
3M Printing and Publishing Systems
3M Center Bldg. 223-2N-01
St. Paul, MN 55144
(612) 733-3497

Cromalin
Du Pont Co.
External Affairs Dept.
Wilmington, DE 19898
(302) 992-4217

Digital Copiers/Interfaces

Canon Color Laser Copier
Canon USA
One Canon Plaza
Lake Success, NY 11042
(516) 488-6700

Colorbus Interface
Colorbus
17975 Skypark Circle, Suite B
Irvine, CA 92714
(714) 852-1850

ColorEdge 1550
Eastman Kodak
343 State St.
Rochester, NY 14650
(716) 724-4000

DocuTech Production Publisher
Xerox Corp.
101 Continental Blvd.
El Segundo, CA 90245
(800) 822-8221

Fiery Controller
Electronics for Imaging, Inc.
950 Elm Ave., Suite 300
San Bruno, CA 94066
(415) 742-3400

Lionheart
Eastman Kodak
343 State St.
Rochester, NY 14650
(716) 724-4000

Imagesetters

BirmySetter
Birmy Graphics
255 East Dr., Suite H
Melbourne, FL 32904
(407) 768-6766

ColorSetter
Optronics
7 Stuart Rd.
Chelmsford, MA 01824
(508) 256-4511

Linotronic Series
Linotype-Hell
425 Oser Ave.
Hauppauge, NY 11788
(516) 434-2744

SelectSet Series
Agfa Corp.
200 Ballardvale Street
Wilmington, MA 01887
(508) 658-6500

Varityper 5000 Series
Varityper, Inc.
11 Mt. Pleasant Ave.
East Hanover, NJ 07936
(201) 887-8000

Printers

BubbleJet
Canon USA
One Canon Plaza
Lake Success, NY 11042
(516) 488-6700

ColorScript Model 10
QMS Inc.
1 Magnum Pass
Mobile, AL 36619
(205) 633-4300

LaserJet/DeskJet Series
Hewlett-Packard
19310 Pruneridge Ave.
Cupertino, CA 95014
(800) 752-0900

LaserWriter/StyleWriter
Apple Computer
20525 Mariani Ave.
Cupertino, CA 95014
(408) 996-1010

Phaser III PXi
Tektronix Inc.
P.O. Box 1000
Wilsonville, OR 97070-1000
(800) 835-6100

Platesetter
Printware
1385 Mendota Hts. Rd.
St. Paul, MN 55120
(612) 465-1400

PM48 Notebook Printer
Citizen America Corp.
2450 Broadway Suite 600
Santa Monica, CA 90411-4003
(310) 453-0614

Scanners/Digitizers

Color Imaging Systems
Barneyscan Corp.
1125 Atlantic Ave.
Alameda, CA 94501
(415) 521-3388

Dycam Model 1
Dycam Inc.
9546 Topanga Canyon Blvd.
Chatsworth, CA 91311
(818) 998-8008

LS-3510
Nikon Inc.
623 Stewart Ave.
Garden City, NY 11530
(516) 222-0200

ScanMaker Series
Microtek Lab
680 Knox St.
Torrance, CA 90502
(310) 321-2121

ScanJet IIc
Hewlett-Packard
19310 Pruneridge Ave.
Cupertino, CA 95014
(800) 752-0900

SpeedScanner
Array Technologies
7730 Pardee Ln.
Oakland, CA 94621
(415) 633-3000

TZ-3
Truvel Corp.
520 Herndon Pkwy.
Herndon, VA 22070
(703) 742-9500

UC Series
Umax Technologies
2352 Walsh Ave.
Santa Clara, CA 95051
(408) 982-0771

VIP 640
Ventek Corp.
31336 Via Colinas, Ste. 102
Westlake Village, CA 91362
(818) 991-3868

Other Products

Bernoulli Drive
Iomega Corp.
1821 West 4000
South Roy, UT 84067
(801) 778-1000

Pantone Matching System
Pantone, Inc.
55 Knickerbocker Rd.
Moonachie, NJ 07074
(201) 935-5500

PrecisionColor Calibrator
Radius, Inc.
1710 Fortune Dr.
San Jose, CA 95131
(408) 434-1010

Radius Two-Page Display
Radius, Inc.
1710 Fortune Dr.
San Jose, CA 95131
(408) 434-1010

Index

About the Authors

James Cavuoto is the editor and publisher of Micro Publishing Press, a publishing company dedicated to electronic publishing located in Torrance, CA. He serves as editor and publisher of *Micro Publishing News,* a regional desktop publishing newspaper with editions in Northern and Southern California, and *Micro Publishing Report,* an industry newsletter for electronic publishing vendors. He is the author or coauthor of several books, including *Laser Print It!, Inside Xerox Ventura Publisher, The Scanner Book,* and *Linotronic Imaging Handbook.* Mr. Cavuoto holds an engineering degree from Case Western Reserve University. He was previously the editor of *Lasers and Applications* magazine, and also a corporate editor for Hughes Aircraft Company in Los Angeles.

Stephen Beale is the executive editor of Micro Publishing Press, serving both *Micro Publishing News* and *Micro Publishing Report.* He is the author or coauthor of several books, including *The Scanner Book, Linotronic Imaging Handbook,* and *Color Image Editing on the PC.* Mr. Beale holds a journalism degree from Temple University. He is the recipient of several writing awards, including recognition from the Newsletter Association and the Computer Press Association. He served previously as senior editor of *Hispanic Business* magazine.